MORE THAN ALL THE GLORIES

A MEMOIR OF LOVE AND REDEMPTION

NATE EDMONDS

Heart's Cry
Publishing

MORE THAN ALL THE GLORIES by Nate Edmonds
Published by Heart's Cry Publishing

www.nateedmonds.com

This book or parts therefore may not be reproduced in any form, stored in a retrieval system, or transmitted in any form by any means – electronic, mechanical, photocopy, recording, or otherwise – without prior written permission of the publisher, except as provided by United States of America copyright law.

Cover Design: Nolan Manning

Cover Photo: Austin Muschamp

Other Photography: Danielle Castle, Jenn Feagans

Headshot: Elizabeth Wiseman

Edited By: Dianna Nash

Contents

Indicates chapters that coincide with songs from the MORE THAN ALL THE GLORIES music project.

THANK YOU....

God of grace and love. It's for Your glory and fame that we live and move and have our being. Thank You for the gift of Your only Son. Thank You for the journey. Thank You for the love and goodness. Thank You for the redemption. And yes.... Thank You for the trial and pain. This is all for You. Every word, every tear, every battle, every triumph, every heart ache, every breathe - for Your glory, by Your grace.

Dana, the strength of your spirit and courage in the fight has forever inspired thousands of people. You were a devoted wife and mother, the catalyst of the story, and a light that shined brighter than you ever knew. Your wisdom and love for Jesus still inspires us all. I am eternally grateful for our nearly nineteen years together. You taught me and the kids so much. You loved like it was all you had to give. This book is dedicated to your honor. I can only imagine the sights you've seen on your new journey.

I could fill the pages of this book with thanks to the precious folks that loved, encouraged and prayed for us along this journey. If you are one of those dear friends, please see this entire story as a thank you letter to you and the God that saw us through. I couldn't possibly name each one of you, but please know that I will never forget your kindness. There are a few however, that I must honor.

Thank you, Dave and Joyce Meyer, Dan and Nicol Meyer, David and Shelly Meyer, Doug and Laura Holtzmann, Steve and Sandra McCollom,

Mike and Pennie Shepard, and everyone at Joyce Meyer ministries. I don't know where my family would be without you. You sustained us financially, spiritually and emotionally through the darkest season of our lives. We will always love and cherish you as family.

Thank you, Pastor Marc and Heidi Sikma and all of our brothers and sisters from Matthias' Lot Church. I am amazed at all you guys did for our family. I have never seen a church body give so much, work so hard and love so sincerely. The memories we share are a true blessing to me. There's not a day that goes by that I don't thank God for you. You were our shelter in the storm.

Thank you, Kile Bay, Jon Shell, Jason Scott, Jason Sarino, Brandon Castle and Jason Low. You guys were true brothers in my deepest pit and will forever be my brothers.

Thank you, Troy Hedman. Your guidance from up ahead of me on the trail was priceless. I made it man... to the beach. It's as beautiful as you said it would be.

Thank you, John Eldredge. I wouldn't be the man I am today without *Wild at Heart* and the many other works you've published. But most importantly, I thank you for taking the time to pray and prophesy over me. Your words for me from Jesus that day may have saved my life.

That covers the front half of the story. But the redemption side has another list of heroes.

Thank you, Pastor Erik and Christ Lawson, Pastor Nathan and Diane Elder, Pastor Leo and LaDawna Crosby, and all of my Element Church Family. You guys picked me up and dusted me off. You have given my family a place to heal and grow far beyond our hopes and expectations. I can dream big again and know that God has brought us into a beautiful season of harvest. Thank you for believing in and supporting this project. It means so much to me to know we are home.

Thank you to my amazing worship staff and volunteers. I am more than humbled to serve with you each week. Nick Giuffrida, Nichole Morrissey, Isaac Boedeker, Harrison Gamber, and Dan Leach, you guys encourage and challenge me every day.

A special thank you to Dianna Nash, for the endless hours you poured into editing these pages. You made me so much better. I could not have done it without you!

Thank you, Keith Harris for always believing in me and putting my heart to music. You are the little brother I never had. We did it, man. We pulled off the nearly impossible project once again. I will always admire your heart, talent, excellence and faithfulness.

Thank you to my Parents, Brenda and Jesse Edmonds, my 4 sisters, Christine, Shelly, Shannon and Tracy, their husbands, Matt, Joe, Jamie and Mike, all my nieces and nephews, Mat, Emilee, Jeremy, Josh, Joey, Jess, Nick, Bella Boo and Dom. I was so overwhelmed, but knowing you were there for us meant everything. I love you all. A special thanks to Shannon and Shelly…. the twins. You two were there for me every time. In the darkest moments and mornings where I didn't know if I could make it another day. The panic attacks and frantic phone calls for help, and of course, picking up the pieces after the storm. I will never forget everything you did.

Thank you to my five beautiful children. I love you all more than you will ever know. You stretch and grow me in ways I could never have imagined you would.

Owen, the eldest and first born. You are a true leader. Stronger and smarter than you know but kinder hearted than most. Who knows where your drive and talent will take you? I will always be proud of you. Stay humble and follow Jesus, that "sunshine in your heart." I'll never forget when you said… "Nate treats me like I am his own son." It changed me forever.

Zach, you are courageous, brilliant and hilarious. I was amazed at your strength during the battle and your ability to hear the voice of God. You are so kind and thoughtful. I will always be proud of you. Never forget who you are. Never ignore the music in you. Don't let yourself get frustrated my son, God is always with you.

Zoe, you are beautiful, intelligent and fierce – a warrior princess. You never back down from a challenge, but you are all together sweetness when you let your guard down. I will always be proud of you. Use your strength wisely my love. Sometimes your gentle spirit will get you farther. You will always be my little girl.

Mason James, the warrior, fearless one. Always ready to take on whoever gets in your way. You are the quintessential boy. Scraped up knees, baiting hooks, and running hard at life. I love seeing you come alive when we play music. I will always be proud of you. Let your brave heart ignite and love well my boy.

Finally, Miss Heidi Lynn. Sissy Boo Boo, the song bird, the fiery headed princess. Your giggles are the best thing ever. I love when you greet me in the morning or hug me before dinner and call me Nate, Nate. I will always be proud of you. Never lose your spark for life. There are so many people you could touch with your smile.

Saving the best for last, my precious Amy. I pray you never forget your vital place in the story. The wounds you've helped to heal in my soul are countless. You stood by my side and believed in me when I lost belief in myself. Knowing you were by my side kept me from utter despair. Your passion and fierce love push our family forward every day. Your beauty inside and out, is something I will never cease to marvel at and question why I was chosen to be given such a prize. I love you more than you will ever comprehend. You are the fireworks. The grand finale'. My love.

INTRODUCTION

Dear Reader,

I am overjoyed that you have decided to take this journey with me and experience all that the Father has written within my family's story. God has taken us to the highest of heights and the lowest of lows – each extreme wrapped in the embrace of His goodness. Because of that goodness, this is not a sad story full of lamenting or bitter questions. Rather, it's a celebration of His faithfulness in all seasons of life. God is faithful on the mountain tops when life is full. But oh, how sweet His comfort in the dark valleys of grief and sorrow.

If you want to truly feel the weight of this journey, as you read, I would encourage you to listen to the music project I have recorded under the same title, "More Than All the Glories." Each song has a corresponding chapter in this book that will tell the story behind the song and bring life to the melodies and lyrics. These songs have been a true source of joy to me in each season they were written.

So, why do this? Why write out this journey and relive it all? I've asked myself this question a lot. At times I've felt like running as far from this story as humanly possible. It's still so shocking this has become my family's lot. Yet, when the storm started to clear, I could see the Father's hand rebuilding our lives from the ashes of our past. I couldn't stay silent. I felt like our story had to be told for a greater good. My silence has been replaced with a greater purpose to share all that God did and continues to do in us, and through us.

I have to testify to the fact that even in times of wandering, loss and longing, Jesus was glorified in our life. He was our joy in the sadness.

I have to tell the brutal truth of what our family experienced but reveal the Father's plan and redemption in it all. Redemption is the only way to describe it. So much brokenness and raw life experience, all mended together in this thing we lovingly call our "new life". I don't have all the answers; in fact, all I can do is boast in the Lord's goodness. But I know the Father has called our family to this story.

I pray that my family's journey will help other hearts settle into the reality that we can only make it through the trials and suffering life will surely bring by resting in God's wondrous grace.

I am asking the Father to use our story to remind us all that following Jesus does not mean life will be easy. But we have hope in Christ. Grace is never more alive in God's children than when He is being glorified through us. It's why we exist.

So, here I am, trusting in His grace alone for the strength to tell our story of love and redemption.

for His glory…. by His grace

THE COMPASS

By Nate Edmonds, Josh Bronleewe and Tedd T
(From the More than All the Glories Worship Project)

You are sovereign, You uphold us
All sufficient, You are
All my striving, All my doubting
I surrender to You
I will trust in You, I will trust in You
Everlasting to everlasting
You are faithful, never changing
In my weakness, when I wander
Guide me spirit, forever You are
You're the compass for my wandering heart
In the waiting, In my questions
You're the answer, You are
All my worry, All my troubles
I surrender to You
I will trust in You, I will trust in You
Everlasting to everlasting
You are faithful, never changing
In my weakness, when I wander
Guide me spirit, forever You are
You're the compass for my wandering heart
In my wandering, In my wilderness
You are the rescue, You're my compass
The compass for my wandering heart

Chapter 1

THE COMPASS

For you are my rock and my fortress;
and for your name's sake you lead me and guide me;
Psalm 31:3 *(English Standard Version)*

June 2014, the house was buzzing with chaos. The construction crew was in full swing. I was running up and down the stairs for supplies, drenched in sweat and dust. As I dug through moving boxes for tools, Zach, my eight-year-old little boy, asked a peculiar question.

Video game controller in hand, not looking away from the TV he said, "Daddy, what's cancer?"

"Um, I don't know son. It's bad cells that grow in your body then turn into a disease."

Zach and his six-year-old sister, Zoe, had escaped the madness of moving and renovations by taking refuge in the basement. I had set up a television and unpacked some of their toys, so they could have a place to play. Zoe was content with her dollhouse and a few stuffed animals. Zach would play video games all day if I'd let him. Sprinting back up the stairs to what looked like a war zone in our soon to be new kitchen, I didn't think much about Zach's question.

We had just moved our family into an eighty-year-old house in the historic city of Saint Charles, Missouri. Before we could unpack, we had to renovate the entire first floor. A frenzy of activity had begun as we completely demoed the kitchen. It was a mess. A few minutes later I came downstairs to rummage for more supplies.

Again, a cancer question, "Daddy, how do you get cancer?"

Standing at the base of the stairs, I said, "Hmm, well, it just kind of happens Buddy. Your cells go crazy, and the cancer takes over."

Over and over again for an hour or so, every time I'd come downstairs - another question.

"Daddy, what does cancer feel like?"

"Does cancer hurt, Daddy?"

"Is cancer contagious?"

Now, Zach was a bit of a hypochondriac in those days. There was always some new condition he thought he had contracted. After a few rounds of questions, I got a little frustrated with him. Why was he asking me about cancer now? I had to hustle through my days off to get this old house into a livable condition. We needed to unpack. I did not have time to talk about cancer. His final question put me over the edge....

"How do you know when you have cancer, Dad?"

I blurted, "Zachary, you don't have cancer! Whatever you're thinking just stop it! You don't have cancer Buddy."

In my stress and frustration, I cut him off. I didn't stop to hear what he was trying to say. I assumed he was being silly, thinking he had cancer. We had a big job to do. I didn't have time for that.

3

Sadly, that was the case a lot back then. I was always on a mission of some sort. I could never seem to just be in the moment. I was looking ahead with the hope that someday, I'd be in a place to stop and enjoy what God had given me. He had given me so much. I had a beautiful wife, Dana, two precious children and now, this cozy old house. I was living my childhood dreams - traveling, leading worship in arenas, and writing songs through *Fuzed Worship,* a group I had co-founded through Joyce Meyer Ministries. I was in my twentieth year of full-time service with the ministry and seeing amazing things unfold. But, when would it be enough? When would that "someday" come when I could pause and enjoy the Father's goodness in my life?

Zack and Zoe continued playing in the basement. I went on to finish the day's work. The kitchen was a disaster. Old houses have plaster and lathe walls that crumble into big chunks of concrete and sand when they are hit with a sledge hammer. Hard hats, goggles and masks were required for safety. Every time I would pound those walls with the hammer, the kitchen became a bigger mess. It was a huge project. I had never taken on anything near that magnitude before.

Dana came and stood in the rubble with me.

"I'm in over my head Babe. I don't have a clue what I'm doing here."

"You'll figure it out. God has a plan. Now, let me try swinging this hammer!"

She took a swing and busted a huge hole in the wall.

"Ooh…this is fun, but way too dirty for me. Please be careful."

And off she went to set up her upstairs office. She could never sit still for long. She was always on a mission to get things done. I knew I was in way over my head. But she was right. God had led us here. He did have a plan. Our little family was in a season of total transition. It felt like we were approaching some major shifts and turns in our life together. This required me to trust the Father. I had to follow His leading into the unknown. In all honesty, trusting in the unknown was a challenge for me. It was a consistent struggle in my spiritual journey. God has always been faithful and yet, at times, I would still doubt His goodness. I would wonder if He'd come through.

I had just written a song in Nashville called "The Compass." It was so fitting for this season of transition Dana and I were in. It was like the Father was speaking through the song. The winds of change were blowing us into an entirely new direction. I thought we were coming out of a wilderness season and into a real harvest. Despite my wrestling with trust, we needed God to guide us. He was the compass pointing due North, keeping the ship of our destiny on course. The words in the song, "You are sovereign, You uphold us," oh how I needed to believe them in my heart.

The Father had always spoken to me, since I was a little boy. That compass in my spirit kept me following His will. But where was He taking my family now? We hoped we were coming into the St. Charles community to serve them and be a light to this old city. Nothing we were doing made sense to Dana's or my natural minds. But in our spirits, we knew we were on a new journey with God. He was stretching us.

We had built our dream house just two exits off Highway 70 from Element Church, a church we had helped plant and served faithfully for eight years. But three years after that move, we felt God asking us to leave the comfort of Element for Matthias' Lot, a smaller church in the heart of the City of St. Charles. This church was thirty minutes from our house. Many of its members live in close community. In fact, most of them moved to the city to be near fellow members and do life together. Their main service was on Wednesday night, so that on Sunday, they could meet in homes all across the city, eat a meal together, and study God's word.

Matthias' rhythm and schedule were such a foreign concept to us, but Dana and I fell in love with everything about it. We so admired the way they lived in fellowship and simplified their lives. We knew God was calling us there. Like so many of the members at Mathias, we felt called to sell our dream house, simplify our lives, and move to the city. We could feel the compass of our spirit leading us there. We became almost obsessed with looking at little one-hundred-year-old houses in a specific zip code, 63301. Dana and I were in such deep agreement as we discussed major changes, we wanted to make in our life together. We thought at times we had lost our minds. Our parents did too. Why would we sell our dream house in suburbia with a three-car garage and trade it for an old house with a detached one car garage or no garage at all?

Our parents asked, "Aren't the suburbs safer than St. Charles City?"

Dana and I would talk for hours at night after the kids went to bed.

Dana would say, "Are we crazy?"

"How much money are we going to lose on this deal?" I would ask.

We would get our phones out and search online, 63301. The houses we were looking at were half the size of ours, yet we couldn't wait to live in them. We just had to be in the heart of St. Charles.

Dana and I prayed for God to find us the perfect home in St. Charles. Since I was about to leave on a trip to the Ecuadorian jungle with Matthias, we thought we'd get everything done to list the house before I left. Then we'd really focus on finding a buyer and a new house when I got back.

Bravely, we planted a For Sale sign in what had been our dream home's front yard. But the Father had a plan to move us quickly.

The first week the sign was in the yard, the house sold. Despite a very slow market, the first person that walked in, bought our house. Dana was frantically trying to negotiate the price and complete the paperwork without me. On my first call home after leaving the states, Dana pleaded with me to find a way to check my email and sign the digital papers quickly, so we didn't lose the contract. The second the church team left the jungle, I rushed to an internet café and signed the digital documents. It was a great conformation that Christ was our compass, and He was guiding us.

Through a series of stressful events - finding a house, getting outbid, searching day and night for another house - we finally found a home. A beautiful, little blue house right in the heart of Saint Charles. Within a month, we had sold our house and moved right into the zip code the Father had put in our hearts, 63301.

After the move, we had about 10 people from Matthias' Lot in our home at all times. We were painting, unpacking and hanging out with new found friends. We had worship nights on the back porch and began to disciple young adults from Matthias. I remember Dana peeking out through the small kitchen window as we sang in the night. I'll never forget how she smiled at me and seemed so at rest. Even in the chaos of a move and construction, with boxes to the ceiling, this was right. It was the start of a new, simpler life. We loved it. She and I had weathered so many trials in our eighteen years together. We were feeling settled in our journey now, firmly focused on relationships with fellow believers and a deeper walk with Christ. Family became a priority over work and ministry.

The little blue house was about a mile and a half from the church. Within five miles in any direction there were church families that we were in community with. Surrounded by people that loved our family, we would do anything to serve one another. We had such anticipation for what the Father could do with us there. What would we get to be a part of? How would He use us to glorify Him? What was the purpose of all these changes and simplifying our life? Our family was on a mission and something big was coming. We could feel it. But what was coming was not what we were expecting.

Less than a month after the big move, with no kitchen or floors, construction dust and boxes everywhere, we got the shock of our lives. A raging tempest crashed with a fury upon the foundation of this new life.

WHAT I KNOW

By Nate Edmonds

(From the More than All the Glories Worship Project)

I stand on the edge of the unknown
Wounded from battle ad scarred
Fighting for love and redemption
Longing for peace in my heart
It feels like the blessings that I count
Have all been burned up in this fight

But what I know is you are faithful
What I know is you are near
What I know is You are able
I rest in You sovereign plan
I reach for Your promises

Behind me the peace of the valley
Before me the mountain I fear
Counting the cost of ascension
Losing what I hold so dear
It feels like the blessings hat I count
Have all been burned up in this fight

Jesus hold me now
Spirit lead me now

Chapter 2

WHAT I KNOW

And he is before all things,

and in him all things hold together.

Colossians 1:17 (ESV)

July 14th, 2014, I heard these dreadful words…. "Well Nate, there's a huge tumor in there. I'm 99% sure it's cancer. She's young, so we'll treat it aggressively. But I'd start the prayer chain."

That was it. The doctor walked out.

Dana was still coming out of anesthesia. The nurses were pulling a camera out of a tube in her throat. As she came to, she looked at me in terror, with tears running down her face, "Did he say cancer?"

All I could do was hold her as she melted into a puddle of grief in my arms. The panic and a thousand questions that ran through my mind put me in a state of shock that lasted the next few days. I was numb, and completely lost. I couldn't show her my fear. I had to be strong. But I could not believe this was happening.

"Father, where are You? I've lost my compass."

As the days went on, the hospital staff tried to figure out what to do next. Dana had originally gone into the doctor with trouble swallowing food and shortness of breath. She had only had these issues for a few weeks, so we hoped it was an ulcer or something else small. There was test after test, doctor after doctor. In the first few days we held on to that one percent the first doctor gave us. He was "99% sure it was cancer." We pleaded with the Father. Stood in faith for that one percent chance. But the tests revealed it was 100%, Stage 3, Esophageal Cancer. After three days of bad news, followed by more bad news, my state of shock came crashing down. It was 5:00am and doctors were rushing into our room like it was noon. Dana couldn't eat. She was fading fast. As they prodded her with needles and tubes, she ran into the small bathroom in her hospital room to vomit.

I finally broke down. I held her tight and wept like a child. "I can't lose you. You've been my life for eighteen years."

Of course, she was in no condition to comfort anyone, so in a typical Dana "tough love" fashion she said, "Nate, you can't do this. I need you to be my rock."

I knew she was right. I had to be strong for her. I asked her to give me 10 minutes. I ran out of the room and down the hall like a sprinter. I don't know where I thought I was going. I just needed to run. I was looking for a place to hide my face and scream out whatever grief was about to erupt in me. The only place of solitude I could find was a bathroom stall. I dropped to my knees and cried so hard I couldn't breathe. The questions and confusion of it all flooded my soul. I was unable to get ahold of myself, so I grabbed my phone and hit the speed dial for Mike, a pastor on staff at Joyce Meyer Ministries. He answered, but I couldn't speak. He could hear me wailing on the other end of the line. He just sat with me.

12

Mike said, "I hear you Nate. I'm with you. You're not alone. I'm with you, Brother."

Mike had been my mentor for several years. He knew how to calm the storms in me with words of encouragement and prayer. We prayed together until I got control of my emotions. I'll never forget that moment, or the many after it where all I could do was break. I remember walking back down the hall, opening the door to Dana's hospital room and pretending my collapse never happened. I would be her rock if it killed me.

The next day, Mike felt he had a word from God for Dana and me that we stood on through the battle, and that I still stand on to this day.

Mike said, "The Father says to rest in His sovereignty, but reach for His promises."

This word was life giving. It confirmed all that was in our hearts. It was like the Father brought together a trust in His sovereign will, but also, a faith I had learned about in my childhood - believe for healing. It meant we could trust that God had us no matter what the outcome. Simultaneously, we could reach for His promise that He was our healer. He would work this together for our good. That word was crucial to our peace in the storm. If God healed Dana here on earth, His promises were true. But if He took her home, His promises were still true. If He took her home, I could rest in His sovereign plan. I could trust that He had us and was at work in our life. He was good. He was faithful. She was healed either way. Either in the light of eternity or here on earth.

As friends and family everywhere began to pray, this revelation came to us. When it felt like the things we counted as the blessings of God were being burned up in the fight, it was what we knew to be truth that held us together. No matter what the circumstances said, God is always faithful.

13

After several days, the hospital sent us home for a bit. Well, what was left of our home. Since most of the little blue house was being demoed and destroyed for construction, we realized pretty quickly our plans had to change. Living in a construction zone during cancer treatments would be impossible. Our new church community from Matthias' Lot sprang into action.

A family going on vacation offered to let us stay in their home for a week. People that barely knew us were offering their home to our family. I was so thankful because it bought me time. I had one week to pull the little blue house together and get a livable situation for Dana to come home to after chemo. Construction workers, volunteers and I descended on that house like an army. I begged and pleaded with granite companies and suppliers to drastically speed up their process. I was trying to do things that would normally take a month, in one week. More people were volunteering their time and God gave my family favor. It was amazing to see. We were really going to pull it off. We'd have the kitchen, and all the old wood floors finished in a week.

The community our family thought we were coming to serve was now serving us. This was really tough for Dana and me. More humbling than I ever realized it could be. We had always served in ministry and gave all we could of our time. Having to let others serve our family really hit us hard. It required more trust – trust I wasn't sure I had to give. But we were in such a desperate situation, we didn't have a choice. We had to sit back, be served, and pull out of all ministry.

I had several big dates coming up for the Joyce Meyer Ministries tour. There was no way I could make them happen and care for Dana. The Meyer family was incredibly gracious. They not only encouraged me to take an indefinite leave of absence but agreed to pay my full salary and every cancer bill while I was gone. That was a blessing I could never repay. In the end, it kept our family from certain financial disaster. We were astonished at all the generosity God had granted us. He wasn't taking the cancer away. But He was proving He was with us in the storm.

While we were staying in our church friend's home, we decided it was time to tell the kids. We sat them down on the bed and broke the news as gently as possible. Their little hearts were flooded with questions.

"Is mommy going to die?" Zoe asked first.

I said, "No, Mommy will be really sick for a while. She will have a big surgery, but it will be ok."

Zachary was pretty silent at first.

I said, "Buddy, what's going on? What are you thinking?"

He just sat back and very calmly said, "I knew it was coming, Dad. I tried to tell you. God told me."

I said, "What are you talking about, Zach? What do you mean, you tried to tell me?"

He said, "In the basement, Dad. I tried to tell you."

Then it hit me. He did try to tell me. But I was too busy to listen. My heart broke.

He said, "Daddy, I tried to tell you. I knew God told me Mommy had cancer."

I said, "Zach, I'm so sorry. You mean to tell me all those questions when I was working that day weren't about you? You didn't think you had cancer?"

15

He said, "No, Daddy. God told me Mommy was going to get sick and that it was cancer, but we'd be ok. I didn't know what cancer meant, so I kept asking you questions."

We just sat and cried. How could this be? I mean, if he just said God had already told him, Dana and I could brush it off as a kid thing. But It wasn't just a kid thing. We had evidence that God really spoke to Zach. It was weeks prior to the diagnosis that this whole cancer conversation happened. This was proof that little Zach really heard from God. It was a astonishing confirmation that the Father had Dana and I, and He had our little ones. He was already preparing their tender hearts for what was to come.

As Dana and I waited for answers and a plan from the doctors, we decided it might be a good idea to get a family photo taken. We didn't know if the treatments would take Dana's hair. She wanted to have a picture of us all together while she looked healthy.

The pain of the tumor in Dana's chest was setting in. She would squeeze my hand between shots, then smile for the next picture.

Holding back tears she leaned in and whispered to me, "Will this be our last family photo?"

I hugged her, "I don't know sweetie. The only thing I know for sure is that God is with us."

FOR YOUR GLORY, BY YOUR GRACE

By Nate Edmonds, Benji Cowart, and Tony Wood
(From the More than All the Glories Worship Project)

If I'm poured out, an offering
Let it be for Your majesty
If I'm broken and You shatter me
Make these ruins Your masterpiece
Make these ruins Your masterpiece

For Your glory, By Your grace
Holding nothing
I'm Yours to take
It's my joy to Surrender all my days
For Your glory, By Your grace

Let my singing, this love I feel
In my suffering grow louder still
Hands are lifted in peace and pain
For You are faithful in everything
Oh, You are faithful in everything

Though we fall down like seeds You've planted
Our hope is held by Your perfect love
There will be a resurrection
And at the harvest we will rise up

Chapter 3

FOR HIS GLORY, BY HIS GRACE

For it is all for your sake,
so that as grace extends to more and more people
it may increase thanksgiving, to the glory of God.
2 Corinthians 4:15 (ESV)

Before the big move, before the cancer and all the trials it brought with it, I heard the voice of the Father so clear. It was January 1st, 2014 – New Year's Day. The dream house in suburbia was filled with the normal mid-day sounds, the TV blaring cartoons, the kids were playing with toys in the living room. I was sitting on the couch taking in all God had done in 2013. I began pleading for more in the coming year. In my pleading with the Lord, I had one request - give me a moto for our family. A creed we could hold up as our mission. I don't know why that request was in my heart. I had never pursued something like that, but our family was on mission. We were charting new territory. I needed a battle cry to rally the troops. The Father quickly answered, "For His glory, by His grace."

19

That was it. So simple and precise. I knew God had spoken that phrase to me. I was so excited. It felt like the purpose of our life was perfected in those words. Yes! Of course! For His glory, by His grace! My song writing, touring and recording projects were finally coming to fruition. Dana had started a new business that was developing. Things were finally about to take off or us. God was about to really bless our life and ministry. We'll do it all for His glory and by His grace.

In my arrogant drive in that season of life, I minimized the gravity of these faithful words. I thought it must be about our new endeavors, our success. We had been so faithful to do whatever the Father had put in our hands. But there were also many years of testing that had led us this far. At one point in my pursuit of a career in music, that pursuit became an idol in my life that consumed me. I had given it a place of importance in my heart that it should never have had. God asked me to lay it down. He asked me to fast all music for a year. I obeyed. I let the Lord purge all of that selfish ambition out of me. I quit leading worship, quit writing songs. I didn't even listen to much music that year. The result of being obedient and giving God one of my greatest desires was Him giving me Fuzed Worship.

God moved in profound ways to help me realize visions I had in my heart since I was a child. I was now living out one vision through Fuzed Worship. Our family was in a new season of blessing. "For His glory, by His grace" - what else could it mean other than God was about to allow us to truly glorify Him with our success?

I had a plaque made and mounted it in our living room. It would be our family creed. When I shared this new creed with Dana, she quickly caught the vision. She felt the weight of it as well. We both knew these words were very special and straight from the Father. I would stand back and stare at the plaque in wonder. What was the depth and meaning of this creed? Why did it feel so weighty? I knew that we live and exist for God's glory. The only way that's possible is through His grace alone. But living for God's glory in my mind, at that time, did not involve suffering. It did not involve winds of chaos raging upon my sweet family or every dream and ambition we had falling down around us. I didn't know how deeply I would come to depend on that grace. I was simply looking ahead at all the wonderful possibilities in our life and ministry.

Now, just six months later, all those possibilities felt shattered. They felt lost in a sea of cancer and chaos we somehow had sailed into. What of these words, "for His glory, by His grace" now? I knew we were right in the center of God's will, but the weight those words carried didn't seem to be realized within our family's story yet. What was God about to require of us? What would He allow us to do?

You can see from this perspective in our journey just how shocking and jolting a cancer diagnosis was. We were living for God's glory! We were doing all we felt we were called to do! We were on a mission to push forward and succeed in the dreams and visions God had given us! From the heights of our desires and living the life we had always sought after, we couldn't see the big picture. But God knew what was coming. He was giving our family a foundation to stand on, a message from our Father. He was going to use our trials and suffering to draw people to Him in a way that we could never imagine. Quite frankly, in a way that we would never have desired or chosen. In His kindness, He was proving Himself faithful to us by giving us that creed to reflect on. In the midst of the raging storm, we could look back and see His hand at work before the chaos.

We were about to be broken and shattered, poured out as an offering. But God wasn't leaving us. He would be right beside us in the storm. He always is. We now had a choice to make as a family. Would we shrink back in this suffering, tend to our wounds and pray for relief? Or, would we let God be glorified in the strength He would grant us? Would we let the world around us into not only the heights of all we were doing in ministry, but in the valley of cancer and many questions? Dana and I felt so vulnerable. We had never faced anything like this. What if things went terribly wrong? What if we lost our faith and walked away from God in anger? What if Dana didn't make it through? How would that bring glory to God?

Despite the fear and unanswered questions, we stepped out in faith. We were determined to glorify God in this storm. We were being poured out as an offering. The Father was leading us so faithfully in all of this chaos. We were called to this moment, for a purpose. Our family would glorify God, even in cancer. "Though we fell down like seeds He'd planted, our hope was held by His perfect love."

We started posting videos online and letting the world around us into our struggle. Later, when some writer friends and I sat down to write the song "For Your glory, by Your grace", I finally understood. In hindsight, I could see the Father's plan and how He held us secure through our struggles. The depth of this epic creed was forever sealed in my heart. We decided the song should be upward, meaning to God, not about Him. This changed the tile to "For Your Glory, By Your grace." Our hope was that these words would cry out in such depth and brokenness that the listener could feel the weight of how our family was called to live for God's glory. I could now speak to the fact that no matter what the Father asks us to walk through, we can choose to glorify Christ in any circumstance. He never leaves. He works all things together for our good. We live and breathe and exist in His story - for His glory, by His grace.

Chapter 4

THE TEMPEST ROARS

God is our refuge and strength, a very present help in trouble.
Therefore we will not fear though the earth gives way,
though the mountains be moved into the heart of the sea,
though its waters roar and foam,
though the mountains tremble at its swelling. Selah
Psalm 46:1-3 (ESV)

Dana was assigned a team of gifted doctors. We felt she was in the best hands possible. In the next few weeks, many experts would study her case to weigh in on what treatments were available to us. But the cancer wasn't waiting for them to figure things out. It was growing, fast. This horrible disease had graduated to Stage 4, as it spread to her liver and further into her stomach. In the first month, she went from a normal, functioning human being to constant vomiting. It got so bad, so fast, she had to have a feeding tube placed in her small intestine. She could no longer eat or drink. We had a 24/7 routine of feeding her through a tube. I had to clean the system every eight hours. I set alarms to wake me through the night to give her meds and refill the feeding pump. It felt like a nightmare we could not escape.

Dana started a five-week run of heavy chemo and daily radiation as we held on to the hope that surgery could remove what the treatments couldn't kill. Day after day, week after week, Dana and I would drive to the hospital. I had always hated hospitals. Something about the needles and the tubes made me nauseous. I had to quickly get over that to care for her. What used to be a 15-minute drive to the hospital turned into a frantic dash to get there before she got sick. I lost count of how many times we would arrive at the cancer center just in time for her to drop to lobby floor, vomiting blood. It was terrifying to watch. I honestly saw things I never imagined could happen to us. It took everything in me to get Dana to that front door where the doctors could take over. I was helpless. I could not fix her. I could not make this go away. I couldn't even ease the pain or comfort her. So, I did what I could do. I prayed. I prayed and trusted God to wake us from this hell, as I grabbed another vomit bag to fill.

As the tumor grew it began to move into the top of Dana's stomach. That, plus the side effects from the chemo and radiation made her so sick she could hardly move. It was like the kids and I had already lost her. When she wasn't at the hospital, she slept about 20 hours a day. The only hours she was awake, she spent vomiting and crying. There were times she would lay on the floor in our bedroom and scream in pain – "God, take me now." There was nothing I could do to help.

All this chaos raged while I desperately tried to keep our kids from seeing their mom like this. The weight of it shook me to my core. I couldn't let them feel that. After five weeks of heavy chemo and radiation. After five weeks of hundreds of people praying for Dana's healing, the doctors did more

25

tests. We were all believing for great news. We were hoping to hear that the chemo was working, or we were making progress. But that didn't happen. It seemed the treatments had only slowed the cancer down. The radiation had changed the texture of the larger tumor, so that Dana wasn't so nauseous, but it hadn't shrunk the tumor. The treatment would definitely not cure the cancer. It didn't seem like the doctors had much hope for that now. We had a special surgeon take a look at the results of the treatments. The possibility of a surgery removing the tumor was ruled out. The cancer was too big. That took Dana's odds of beating the disease down drastically. The experts told us she had a two percent chance of beating it without a Red Sea sized miracle from God. That was not what we were expecting to hear.

People across the globe began to pray. A team of worshipers would come to the house to sing over Dana every week. We could feel the strength of the Spirit rising in us. But the diagnosis wasn't changing. Given this news, Dana and I began to have a lot of serious talks. The shock of it all was wearing off. The reality of what we were facing was growing heavier and heavier to bear.

As we sat on the back porch of the little blue house one day I said, "What are you feeling in your heart, sweetie?"

I wanted to know if the Father had given her a heads up because I was starting to sense that this journey may not end as we were hoping.

She answered, "God has really strengthened me, Nate. My resolve is set. God has granted me some real faith for this. I feel it like never before. Please, have everyone pray and plead for a miracle because my faith is not for a miraculous healing. It's faith to go through. Maybe God will give us a miracle in the end, but I don't see it right now. I just see Him giving me strength to go through some heavy stuff. I know I am called to glorify Him in this process. For His glory, by His grace, right?"

Even though that was what God was speaking to me as well, it was sobering to hear it from Dana. She was always the eternal optimist. She had received several miraculous healings in her life. I could always look in her eyes and find hope and positivity. But here she was saying we were in for a storm, and the way out was through. I held her tight and told her I knew God was faithful. I didn't understand why this was happening, but I knew God had us. He had set us up for this. He had hemmed us in. We were surrounded with love and support. God was proving His faithfulness to us, even though He was leading us through the valley of the shadow of death.

Throughout our married life, we always had amazing confirmation of what the Father was speaking. Right in the middle of our talk, we received word from a trusted friend, Joyce Meyer.

Joyce said, "Nate and Dana, don't let anyone tell you that Dana won't be healed unless you guys muster up enough faith to heal her. Faith is a gift granted by God. If He wants her healed this side of heaven, He will grant you the faith for that. If not, He will grant you the faith to go through."

It was exactly what God was speaking to us. From that day on, we stood on this truth. Faith came by hearing, and hearing by the word of God. Everywhere we turned, it was the same message, God is in control. He will guide us through the storm.

For by the grace given to me I say to everyone among you not to think of himself more highly than he ought to think, but to think with sober judgment, each according to the measure of faith that God has assigned. Romans 12:3 ESV

God had assigned us a measure of faith. He provided all we needed. This storm was ours to face. Looking back now it's so clear, but in the chaos, it was harder to see. If we had stayed in our dream house, we would have been thirty-five minutes from our faith community. We wouldn't have had all the love and support that sustained us. The best cancer center in the city was just two exits from our new St. Charles home. We were a part of a great community at Element Church. But we were so busy with traveling, kid's activities, and Dana's business our focus was not on fellowship with our brothers and sisters in Christ. Every church has its place in the body, gifts or callings unique to them. Element's vision is reaching people on a mass scale across the entire Saint Louis region.

Matthias' Lot is laser focused on a tight community in St. Charles. In hindsight, I can see that the Father knew what we needed in this season of life. He was sheltering us in so many ways. I used to say, it was like God put pillows around our suffering. Beautiful pillows of love and kindness that we could rely on and lean on in the darkest of nights.

This new community brought us meals four or five days a week. They would run over and baby-sit the kids when I had to rush Dana to the hospital in the middle of the night. They fixed our plumbing and took Dana to appointments when I was sick. There was even a group of ladies that had me train them in all the things I did to care for Dana, so that I could take a day off when I needed to get away. It was truly the Father's goodness all around us.

The more the tempest raged, the more God would lean in through His people. Encouragement came from every side. When we started to feel like we couldn't go on another day, a stream of text messages, phone calls, or online posts would pour in. Meals would come to the house. People would come to work in the yard and serve our family. I had such rich talks on the back porch with men that had become my true brothers. The church was alive and ready to journey with us.

With all of the tough conversations arising, the one we definitely couldn't avoid was "what if?" What if Dana didn't make it through this? What if she went home to be with Jesus? After eighteen years of being there for each other, the kids and I might lose the sun in our universe. God might choose to heal her in heaven, not here on earth.

On the drives to and from the hospital each day, we passed a funeral home. It's a very majestic looking building surrounded by tall trees and beautiful gardens.

Dana would often say, "If Jesus takes me home Nate, that's where I want to be buried."

"Why," I asked. "Why there? There is a place closer to our home we could walk to."

"I don't know, Nate. I'm just drawn to it somehow. I want somewhere peaceful for you and the kids to go. There's something special about that place."

I promised I would make it happen, as she made it clear that she would plan her own funeral. No matter how much I pleaded with her to not worry about those things, to let me handle them, she was determined. She would have a beautiful funeral. She would plan it all herself. Each time she brought it up, I agreed to all her wishes.

She would close her eyes as if it calmed her soul to know that's where her final resting place would be.

Chapter 5

LIVING THE DREAM

Delight yourself in the LORD,
and He will give you the desires of your heart.
Psalm 37:4 (ESV)

One fall morning, I was sitting in the cancer center like I did most days. As I watched the chemo work its way through the pump and into Dana's veins, I couldn't help but think of better times. In the many hours I spent there as a healthy man, in the midst of so many people fighting for their lives, my mind and heart would go to all sorts of places. I had to leave there in my imagination to keep myself sane. If I didn't, the desperation of cancer would overtake me, leaving me weak, unable to be the support that Dana needed. In our almost nineteen years together, we had lived so well. As she closed her blue eyes and slipped into the fog the drugs would put her in, my heart began to dream of the day we met.

"Surfs up, Dude" Dana said with a cheesy smile, as I sat sipping my drink. "You know, cause we're both from the beach?"

"Ah, I get it," I said, trying to play it cool.

Who was this blond-haired surfer girl with blue eyes that beamed as if they had light behind them? A friend had just introduced us at a party, thinking we'd have a lot in common as we had both just moved to Missouri from different coasts - I from Florida and her from sunny California. We were lost in a new sea of preps and cornfields. Looking completely out of place wearing sweat pants with white gym socks sticking out the toes of her Birkenstock sandals, I was certainly intrigued.

"How awful is this weather?" I said.

"I know, I think my skin is getting more and more pale by the day. I haven't seen the sun in weeks," she replied.

As we talked, I couldn't help but notice how she radiated a love for Jesus. We laughed and told stories of our glory days with friends on the beach. I wasn't quite sure what to make of Dana. She was so different than the girls I was used to. Something in me was drawn to her, but it wasn't quite our time. I would keep my eye on her over the next year as we both dated other people and hung out every weekend and Wednesdays at youth group. As the Father would have it, we grew very close the summer after I graduated high school.

I started my career at Joyce Meyer Ministries, touring, playing on the worship team and working in their warehouse. Dana stayed behind as a senior and refused to date anyone. She was focusing on her relationship with Christ, which I loved. But I just knew one day, we'd be together. I patiently waited through the summer as I traveled with the ministry and came home to her waiting for me on the front porch - Daisy Dukes and golden blond hair. Dana couldn't see it yet, but I was certain she would be my wife one day.

Dana and I would talk for hours, laying on the trampoline in her parent's backyard. We'd gaze at the stars, dreaming about all that God might do in

31

our future until the early morning hours. Since she was "dating Jesus," I was stuck in the "friend zone." She was oblivious to my advances. I would always open doors for Dana, comment on her beauty, and bring her gifts home from my trips. Her responses were short.

As I opened the door to the mall for her one day, she finally said, "You don't have to do those things for me. Guys don't do those things for me."

In a desperate attempt to test the waters, see if I could get to her heart I said, "Well, maybe you've just been with the wrong guys."

It fell flat. No response at all. I would forever be stuck in the "friend zone." We were just friends, buddies, besties, and I was furious about it.

The day finally came when I heard the Lord speak. I heard Him so clearly say it was time. My heart began to pound as I carried boxes through the warehouse area where I worked at the ministry. I called Dana on my lunch hour and asked if she could meet me at my parent's house that evening. She acted shy about my request but agreed to be there. Little did I know; the Father was speaking to her as well. Both of our minds were racing at the thought of what might happen that evening. What would I say? What if she wasn't feeling the same things? What romantic, extravagant presentation could I come up with to finally win her heart?

When I got off work, this peace began to settle over me. I knew God was on the move and everything would work out for our good. When I got home to my parent's house, I came up with a simple plan. A romantic stroll through our wooded neighborhood with a simple talk about all the feelings I had been holding in my heart for her. It had to work. It was all I had. I was nineteen and in love.

When Dana arrived, I could tell she was nervous. She knew I was up to something. I asked her to go on a walk with me. She reluctantly said, yes.

Over the next hour, we were both amazed at what was happening. The Father was actually speaking to both our hearts that day. He was speaking the same things to Dana only this was the first time she had thought about me in that way. All the things I was speaking from my heart were exactly what she had been praying God would give her in a relationship. The goals I said I wanted to achieve in our life together were the very things she had been desiring. It was settled. When we could afford it, we would be married, travel the world together in ministry, have two kids (a boy and a girl, boy first) and live happily ever after.

I am still amazed at what we saw in our hearts that night. By the grace of God, it all happened just as we had planned. My Uncle Dan, who was a mentor to me in my twenties, advised me to get a ring on Dana's finger.

He was also convinced she was the one. Within a few weeks I sold the speakers out of my car and used the money to buy her a ring. We dated one year, were engaged one year and were married in October 1996. Over the next ten years, we were inseparable. We drove to work together every day.

Had lunch together every day. We traveled the globe together as I played music for Joyce Meyer Ministries before having Zach and Zoe. A boy and a girl, Zach was first. We wanted a big brother that could protect his little sister. We saw magnificent things in our travels including India, Africa, Australia, Ireland, England, and many of the fifty states. Our marriage wasn't always perfect. We certainly had our ups and downs, but the Father was faithful through it all. He granted us all of our heart's desires.

So many years later, dreaming of our younger years from the cancer center, the Father was still leading us. He was our compass in a new, much more difficult season of life. This was certainly not in our plan or heart's desires. But we could feel the embrace of God's love right in the middle of it. We couldn't understand why we had to face this pain. But we couldn't deny the fact that the compass of our spirit had led us here. This was our lot. Moreover, our calling. We were called to glorify Christ even in the midst of sudden tragedy and disaster. We knew we were called to show the world an unwavering faith in a sovereign God. We had the faith to go through. Jesus was with us. He would never leave or forsake us. He promised it in His word.

Despite the faith that was so clearly granted us, we were still only human. Just as Christ, in His humanity, pleaded with the Father to remove the cup of the crucifixion from Him, we too pleaded. In my walks through Saint Charles to pick the kids up from school, I would have my moments of prayer. I remember one particular day when gut wrenching grief came over me. I wept and cried out to God in the pain. I pleaded with Him to not take Dana from me. If there was any way for this cup of sorrow to be removed from us, I wanted it gone. But as my emotions subsided, I wiped away my tears to hide my pain from the kids. I did not have a clear answer from the Father as to where we were heading, but His peace was with us. That peace saw me through one day at a time.

IRRESISTIBLE GRACE

By, Nate Edmonds, Travis Ryan and Richie
(From the More than All the Glories Worship Project)

Lord, you haunt me
With your relentless love
How could you want me
After the things I've done

Pouring out, pouring out, irresistible grace
Captured by mercy, I stand amazed
Hear the sound, hear the sound, as the broken sing praise
Caught in the grip of Your grace
I'm saved

You pursue me
No matter where I run
Ever-redeeming
All of the things I've done

So, look to the heights of the Calvary hill
Our King on a Cross is fulfilling God's will
His blood like a waterfall washing our sins away

The guilt of our past and the weight of our shame
Undone by the death that the lamb overcame
His blood like a waterfall washing our sins away

Chapter 6

MOMENTS OF IRRESISTIBLE GRACE

Three times I pleaded with the Lord about this,
that it should leave me.
But he said to me, "My grace is sufficient for you,
for my power is made perfect in weakness."
Therefore, I will boast all the more gladly of my weaknesses,
so that the power of Christ may rest upon me.
2 Corinthians 12:8-9 (ESV)

After so many months of battling cancer, Dana and I were certain of one thing, it is only by God's grace that we can press through the trials of life and live for His glory. All we could do was boast in our weakness as we trusted the Lord for strength. Our own strength was grossly insufficient. God was faithful to grant us all we needed. By His grace, we had so much love and support. The harder the battle got, the more God drew us close to put those pillows around our suffering. There were many times when the Father let us know He had us. That somehow, this would all work together for His glory and our good. Our suffering wasn't going away. In fact, it kept increasing. As the stress built in me, it even began to affect my health as illness after illness plagued my body. Doctors could never point to a specific cause. It was simply the stress and grief growing in me that came out in physical ailments.

I had to use a cane for several weeks because my back got so tight that my leg drew up and wouldn't straighten. I couldn't even drive a car. That healed. Then my neck grew stiff. Eventually, I couldn't move my head at all. For a month, I could only move my eyes to see from side to side. I had to use my hand to lift my head off the pillow in the morning because my neck was completely frozen. I started having horrible acid reflux. My chest felt like it was on fire every day. The acid caused me to lose my singing voice for six months. Any attempt to sing came out as a whisper.

The worst ailment I faced was debilitating panic attacks. They lasted for days on end. One attack got so bad. I thought I was having a stroke and had to call for help. The vicious attacks left me in a fog for several days after they subsided. Once I drove into the back end of a car wash thinking it was the entrance. The attendants ran out screaming. They thought I was on drugs. The waves and seas kept crashing upon me. I looked like a different person, thirty pounds heavier and hobbling with a cane.

Yet, there was this irresistible grace. Irresistible grace was a term I had grown fond of in my studies of the doctrines of John Calvin. It's the thought that God's grace is so beautiful and extravagant that the human heart cannot resist it. Although Dana and I had already received our salvation, by grace, through faith - I believe that same grace surrounded us in suffering. God had us, loved us, and sustained us. Strength came from simple moments of irresistible grace. Moments where the undeniable peace and presence of the Holy Spirit would flood our souls. In these moments of grace, we could sense a much greater purpose unfolding by faith. We saw the hand of the Father in our story. I want to share these moments because I believe they reveal His goodness in our story, even when the storm raged on. As hard as these moments were, they let the process of loss settle in softly verses hit us all at once. They broke life down to its simplest form as the chaotic drive of ministry and business became meaningless.

One such moment was the start of a new treatment that would cause Dana to lose her hair. She had the choice to shave it all off or watch it fall out in giant clumps. We tried to involve the kids in as many of these things as we could. This was important for their grief and ability to process as children. Dana and I decided to have a party on the back patio of the little blue house. We asked a few family and friends to come over, then got the razor out. We videoed the whole thing. We even let the kids take the scissors and cut Mom's hair. It was sad and painful. But it was a huge piece of us processing all this as a family. It eased us through the storm, together. Everyone was

39

talking and sharing the moment. It let the grief of what was happening settle in our souls.

All of Dana's golden blond hair fell to the ground that day. Without her hair, Dana definitely looked like a cancer patient. That treatment ended up taking her hair, but we were ready. She became completely bald. We joked and took pictures because our heads looked the same now. I have been slick bald for most of my adult life. But this was definitely not a moment we ever thought we'd share. I can't imagine what it was like for Dana. She had to let go of what the world said was a woman's physical beauty. But she wore her new look proudly. She never once let it get to her. Instead, she bought a lot of hats and scarves. She made the best of it. She was determined to let Christ shine though her no matter how her outer appearance changed. An irresistible grace saw her through.

Throughout Dana's battle, she would ask me to worship with her. We would sing songs in the night when it seemed there was nothing left to hold on to. This gave us many sweet moments of irresistible grace. But during the season where I mysteriously lost my singing voice, worshiping with her hurt. Acid reflux and ongoing sinus infections had silenced my song. It really hurt to try and sing. I had nothing left, but a whisper. That made for such a tender offering to the Lord. In complete brokenness and surrender we would sing at a whisper,

"Oh no, You never let go, through the calm and through the storm."

As hard as it was at times, we had the faith to whisper,

"You're a good, good Father, it's who You are, it's who You are."

And of course, we sang, "It is well with my soul."

Tears streaming down our faces as we worshipped in spirit and truth. We cried out in the shadows as grace washed over us. Looking back, I am amazed at the faith the Father granted.

As much as we pleaded for Dana's healing, we so deeply felt she was going to Heaven soon. The natural circumstances certainly looked bleak. But far bigger than the natural outlook, Dana really felt like this was her time. The fact that we could sing and worship God, knowing He was taking her home is astonishing to me even now. Only the Father could grant that. We couldn't do that in our own strength. Only His irresistible grace surrounding us could produce these moments. Our singing and our devotion to Jesus grew in our suffering. I am forever thankful for that. The Father would strengthen us and give us fuel and endurance, by His grace, for one more day. Like Paul and Silas in jail, we sang in the night.

It was also important for me to take time out to let the kids know I was still there for them. That even though the cancer was making Mommy sleep a

41

lot, Daddy was still strong. I wasn't going anywhere. I needed to guide them through, letting their little hearts breath and process everything that was hitting us.

One day, Zach asked me to teach him to skateboard. On this day, I came to realize all that was going on in him. He had this long flowing hair then. He looked so hard-core on the outside. But inside, his heart was breaking. He got on his little skateboard, but quickly lost control. He couldn't balance on it. That made him furious.

He screamed, "I hate this stupid skateboard. I hate God!"

I said, "Zachary! You do not hate God."

He said, "Yes I do, Daddy! He won't let me learn how to skateboard!"

Wow, I knew there was something much bigger brewing here. This had nothing to do with skateboarding and everything to do with a battle in his little heart.

I pulled him close, "Let's go have a talk, Buddy."

We sat on the curb and started digging into his grief. I told him that it was ok to voice his anger, even at God. God understood his pain and wanted to meet him there.

Zach said, "Daddy, how can I love a God who won't even let me skateboard and.... He's killing my mommy?"

My heart broke for him. I couldn't miss this moment to teach him and point him to the grace of God.

I said, "Zachary, God isn't killing your mommy. Cancer is. Even though we don't understand all of this. We know that God is with us. We have a choice now to glorify Him with our story. You know you don't hate God, Buddy. You've been walking with Him and hearing His voice your whole life. You're His. He bought you with a price. He knew you and had a plan for you even before the He made the earth. But this is a really hard time. There's so much we just don't understand. But God is faithful, Buddy. He loves you and is with you even when it hurts so bad."

I began to tell him of all the people our story was touching. So many people were coming to Christ. The Father was using us to renew their faith. Dana would post a video about seeing the Lord in her suffering and forty thousand people would share or like it.

I said, "Somehow, God has a plan in all this, Zach.

He said, "Really Daddy? I want to see."

I took him in the house. Dana had just woken up. When I told her what had happened, she opened up her laptop and began to show him all the messages we had received. She showed him those people that our story was having a profound impact on for the glory of Christ. Zach's spirit was lifted. His bright eyes and big smile were back. It meant so much for him to see the Father's hand and realize we weren't alone. God had a purpose in all this. Irresistible grace began to fill his heart. I snapped a picture that day of Zach with his skateboard. I found it recently. I'll never forget God's faithfulness to him on one of the toughest days of his life.

At dinner, Zach prayed the sweetest prayer. He prayed that God would allow us to really worship Jesus at church that night. I was amazed at his strength, at how Jesus met him in his grief. We did truly worship that night. Matthias' Lot has the kids stay in the sanctuary with the adults for worship. We held each other and sang to God as a family. One more moment of irresistible grace. The Father was assuring Dana and I that He had us, and He had our little ones.

As the ups and downs of Dana's illness dictated our days, we knew we needed to find a way to make some lasting memories with the kids. Dana really wanted to take them to Disney World one last time before she left them. One of our dear friends heard what she was doing and offered something incredible. She was part of a group called Stella's Wish that granted families like us the funds to make memories. Within weeks we had a large check to cover some of the costs. As word spread that we were going to Disney, checks started showing up in the mail. So many people did unbelievable things. Before we knew it, we were on a plane with an all-expenses paid trip to Disney World.

Before we left for Disney, I was in the basement doing laundry and had one of my moments of grief and anguish with God. I broke down in tears and prayer. I was battling my own anger at Him. I was trying so urgently to understand His plan in all this. The Father began to speak to me clearly. I had some deep questions because a few months prior I had a moment of grace one morning where this extraordinary peace came over me. I knew I always had God's ear, but this was something so different.

That morning I whispered to Him, "Are you going to take my wife?"

In an almost audible voice, I gently heard, in my spirit, "Yes, son, I am."

I whispered, "When?"

All I sensed was, January or February.

This was in December, so I instantly stressed out and that peace was gone. January or February? That was soon. Through counseling I was encouraged to really seek God about that moment. Something wasn't lining up. I needed clarity. Now, in the basement, I felt that peace again. I wanted answers from the Father. I asked Him, what He meant in that moment of peace. I needed clarity.

Once again, He spoke, "Nate, I didn't say I would take her in January or February. I just said that is all you need to focus on. Don't focus on the end. Just focus on the here and now, what is before you."

As I knelt in the floor and wept, God began to reveal what would take place over the next few months. Like a movie in my mind's eye, He revealed that He would bless the Disney trip, which was planned for February. We would have a precious time. Then, there would be a season of ease where things would get into a routine. We would have some sort of new normalcy. But soon after, things would get ugly. Dana's health would begin to decline as her time here on earth would come to an end. I was stunned. I knew I had

45

heard from God. I wanted to have accountability in that. I told only a few faithful brothers what the Father had spoken to me. I did not tell Dana. I didn't want it to affect her fight. I mean, what if I was wrong and this was all a crazy grief delusion? But what if I was right?   What if this was God? I wanted a small group of brothers to be able to testify to it. They could bear witness that the Father was speaking and guiding us in this storm. Only time would tell.

We went to Disney. The trip was certainly not without its cancer issues. There were several times when we were scrambling to figure out solutions for problems with Dana's feeding tube. Thankfully, I brought my sister, Shelly with us. She is a nurse which was a big help with the medical chaos. Dana's mother also came along to help out, as well as to spend some time with Dana. The first few days at Disney were really rough on me. I began to question the Father's "blessing" on the trip. It seemed like things just weren't clicking for us. There were graphic, stressful moments with Dana's health.

The weight of caring for her and the kids away from home just got to me. Once, we had to jump off a moving ride and rush Dana to get medical attention. But, just after all the commotion calmed down, and we got back to our schedule, something amazing happened. We got a text from my 21-year-old nephew Joey, Shelly's son. He was off fighting the war in Afghanistan. He saw horrible suffering there. Things that made him grow up fast. He kept a small camera on his head that captured every moment of his time there. He sent us a picture from the battlefield. It wasn't of guns and tanks, but rather, a symbol of love from one type of battlefield to another. While Dana was fighting for her life, he was fighting for freedom. In the midst of chaos and violence, His entire squad took the time to line up around their armored vehicle. They were holding up a banner. It read, *#danastrong, for you Aunt*

Dana, from Afghanistan. What a surprising gift. It gave us strength to laugh and push through the pain we were feeling. Once again, we had peace in the storm.

That night everyone was exhausted. The kids fell asleep on my chest on the bus ride back to the hotel. It was the first time this thought really sank in. As Dana glanced over at me in tears, I could tell she had the same thought, I was about to be a single dad.

The next morning, I was carrying a tray full of everyone's food. The wind blew the tray over. Everything fell to the ground. I lost it.

I dropped to my knees and cursed at God. "Why Father? Why is this Your will for us? I can't take anymore! You have not blessed this trip. Nothing is going right. How is this Your blessing?"

It's amazing how when I am pushed to my limits, even the smallest thing can set me off. It can make me feel completely defeated. But then God spoke to me. "My blessing son, is that you learn to have peace in the storm."

I said, "Ok God, let's do this then. Be my strength."

I picked myself up. From that moment on I refused to be stressed. My whole outlook totally changed. God honored His word to me. Our trip was blessed. It was a beautiful time.

Dana had planned many special moments. She skipped a few weeks of chemo, which made her able to feel halfway decent. The doctors gave her steroids for each day to boost her energy as well. She had this scooter that she rode around.

The thing was so fast we all had to jog to keep up with her. Dana was on a mission, as usual. Nothing would stop her.

The picture of Dana and the kids riding on her scooter is forever etched in my mind. It broke my heart to watch her cling to them, knowing what they would have to endure after she was gone.

Sometimes God's blessing was not what we wanted it to be. I had to redefine this word, "blessing." I had to trust that the Father was good, even when my heart was breaking. He was good, even when this trip was part of a long sad goodbye. He was good, even when I had to watch my kids ride on a scooter with their mommy because she was slowly dying before their eyes. Even then, I had peace in the storm.

When we got back from Disney, it was just as the Father spoke. We had a season of a "new normal." We were in a standard routine of chemo, then recovery time. Life was a bit more manageable. Dana became passionate about helping kids that were facing a life-threatening battle with cancer. As hard as it was for our family to understand Dana's battle, we couldn't imagine facing it as a child. We met several families that had a child with cancer, through many different circumstances. Each time Dana would have it on her heart to bless them. She began to post online and ask people to partner with her to bless kids with cancer.

Through the Build a Bear Company, Dana arranged for over twenty-five families to donate the funds to Build A Bear for kids with cancer. When she reached that goal, she was so proud. She asked all the families that donated to come build their custom bear for a child with this awful disease. Dana and the kids beamed with joy as the bears were delivered to the hospital. Story after story came in from kids that were blessed with their gift. Even in her suffering, Dana reached out and touched others. Her generosity was a blessing to see, a testimony of God's perfect strength in her. All those kids were touched by God's irresistible grace. It was also incredible for our kids to see that we could be a light to others, even in our own suffering.

There were so many moments of irresistible grace through this journey, little snap shots in time that I will always carry deep in my soul. During those moments, Dana, the kids and I talked of the future and what it would look like without Mommy. By God's grace, we even talked about Daddy re-marrying and what a new family might look like after Mommy was gone. We had weekly counseling that helped the kids sift through their grief and process their feelings.

Dana gave Zach, Zoe and me her blessing to move on. She didn't want us to live in grief. Dana said the Lord spoke to her about our future. In her heart, she knew that I would remarry quickly, that her death would thrust me into a new level of ministry. These moments allowed me and the kids to grieve up front and slowly ease into our world changing after Mommy died. Without them, our road would have been so much harder. When Dana freed us to find a new Mommy, and me to expect a new ministry, she released more of those pillows around our suffering. The Father kept pouring out this irresistible grace. In our brokenness, we could sing praise because He had caught us up in His goodness. We could look to our salvation and the Hill of Calvary, knowing we were secure in Christ.

I know everyone that has lost a loved one has a different story. Ours seems to be beautifully sprinkled with all these signs from God or moments of grace. But one reason our story has these moments is we chose to see them. We chose to sit and connect the dots as we recalled the goodness of the Father. Then, turned to the world around us and lived out that grace with them. The more we glorified God in grace and marveled at His hand in our lives, the more we saw Him at work in us. His grace is sufficient even when He doesn't take away the suffering. I would testify that it's actually in those times of great suffering that we are able to clearly see His hand the most. Seeing grace in the suffering has forced me to lay my pride and business aside. I've learned to truly rely on Him. These *moments of irresistible grace* have led me to repentance and worship of a Holy God. His grace is always sufficient.

Chapter 7

THE END DRAWS NEAR

So, we do not lose heart.
Though our outer self is wasting away,
our inner self is being renewed day by day.
For this light momentary affliction is preparing for us an eternal weight of
glory beyond all comparison, as we look not to the things that are seen but to
the things that are unseen.
For the things that are seen are transient,
but the things that are unseen are eternal.
2 Corinthians 4:16-18 (ESV)

The treatments began to leave Dana in bed for days on end again. The amount of time she was actually able to function and be with our family was significantly limited. She would sleep for almost a week straight. She'd have a couple of days where she was awake maybe three to four hours, then hit another round of chemo to start it all over again. The feeding tube and other multiple issues were also making her quality of life poor. To make matters worse, her blood counts and immune system were so low that she could no longer handle the treatments. The doctors told us they had done everything

53

they could do. They recommended we stop all treatments and let Dana be. We had no choice as the treatments were killing her faster than the cancer.

But the weight of what that meant was overwhelming. It felt like we were letting go of the fight and surrendering. Where would that lead us? What would happen to her body as the cancer grew? How would Dana pass away?

As we prayed, we knew we had to trust the Father to lead us down the path home. Dana and I finally talked about the timeline God had spoken to me. She shared that He had spoken the same things to her. We did the only thing left to do. We stopped all treatment. No more pills. No more needles. No more daily trips to the hospital. It was just us, together as a family, trying our best to find joy in whatever time she had left. Now we would simply live and wait. Wait for Jesus to take Dana's hand and lead her to eternity. The treatments had at least made it possible for her to eat small portions and drink water. But the feeding tube affected her quality of life. She cried, saying how much she hated that thing.

We had to make another dreadful decision. She hadn't used the tube in months. All it caused was horrific pain. She demanded it be removed. But this decision could have deadly consequences. If the cancer grew, it could close that pathway off again, and she would not be able to eat or drink. As we prayed, we had peace in our hearts. I scheduled the surgery.

After the surgery, Dana was liberated. When the wound healed, she could swim! She hadn't been able to be submersed in water for over a year. Every shower she took, I wrapped her abdomen in plastic wrap and tape it off with medical tape like she was a shipping package. It was summer. Dana wanted to make memories. She wanted one last time to swim with the kids. We booked a day at a friend's pool, and we got wet! We jumped and played and took underwater pictures with Mommy. It was definitely a time to remember, a moment of grace. We were thankful for those sweet moments.

Over the course of Dana's battle, she went through different stages of her own grief and accepted what was happening to her. Early on, one of her nurses encouraged her to start leaving notes for the kids, just in case the worst happened. But at the time, she just couldn't bring herself to do it. Eventually, Dana came up with a plan to leave Zach and Zoe all sorts of things.

Dana and I started recording videos for each birthday and Christmas until the kids were in their twenties. A trinket accompanied each video from Mom and a scripture for them to stand on for the year. When the end drew near, the urgency to finish those videos grew stronger. As soon as the chemo effects wore off Dana was on a mission. We had to purchase all the trinkets and have them engraved. Everything had to be meticulously organized, so that I could remember what to do each year after Dana was gone. It was quite an undertaking since she had so few hours to give each day. But with the treatments stopping, we knew we had a short window of time to finish things before Dana would leave us. Day after day she would find the strength to wake up for a bit and pour her heart out to the kids in these videos. It was so precious, but so hard to watch.

As Dana's need for pain medication became more frequent, the kids and I got less hours a day with her. There were times she seemed unconscious but would suddenly wake up and shoot a quick video. She would close her eyes between takes as I prepared the next scripture and trinket for her to hold up and show the kids. She painstakingly guided them through every year of their life, knowing she wouldn't be there in person. Dana wanted to parent them and point them to Christ from eternity. Puppetry, graduation day, wedding day, Dana and I journeyed through Zach and Zoe's lives and trials in advance. It was so amazing to see her strength and diligence as a Mom. I will never forget the example she set for us all.

Dana and I continued to talk about the future for the kids and me. What would I do? How would I raise the kids? When would I remarry? It was so strange to talk to her about my future wife. This just shouldn't be. Even the kids were letting their hearts go into the future. Zoe asked me so matter of fact once, "Well, Dad! You're going to remarry right?

You're not going leave me without a Mommy?"

It was crazy. But it was part of our grieving process. It again, allowed us to grieve early on and not get hit by grief suddenly. Our counselors had encouraged these things to happen. They challenged me to let my heart go to the future as the Lord led - to imagine losing Dana and what it meant. It was foreign at first, but it was so healthy for our souls. This was coming without a miracle from God and there was no changing it. My family had to face it head on, together. Of course, Dana would cry at times, but she so desperately wanted to know where we'd go in the years to come, without her. She just wanted to know that we'd be ok.

I would joke and say, "I'm never going to remarry, Dana. I mean, who wants a forty-year-old bald guy with two kids and a deceased wife. Nobody wants that."

To which she would reply, "I know the ladies will be lining up as soon as I'm gone Nate. You're the best husband a woman could ask for."

As sweet as that was, I highly doubted she was right and marrying another woman seemed a million miles away from our current state. My plans were - a truck, a dog, and a trip. I had always wanted a truck, and I thought a dog would really help the kids through their grief. A trip with just the three of us seemed like a peaceful thing to do after Dana was gone. I got online and found the perfect dog - a big, fluffy Goldendoodle. There was a liter that would be born soon.

I found a breeder that was kind enough to drive an hour to our home, so Dana could meet the mommy dog and see what our dog might look like. She held back tears as she pet the dog, imagining us without her. Dana also wanted to pick out my truck and see me in it. I looked online for weeks finally finding the right one. I showed her a picture online, and Dana loved it. I bought it the next day, so she would have a chance to ride in it. It brought her so much joy to see that dog and that truck. She just wanted to know there was some form of peace and joy coming for us in her absence. It was shocking. It was hard to wrap our heads around. But this was our life. We had to make the most of it.

As friends and family got word that we were stopping treatments, many people wanted to come say their goodbyes and be with Dana. At least twelve hours of each day were spent with people coming in and out of the little blue house. They brought gifts and food. Some just wanted to care for us. It was a pretty amazing thing to experience, but it was also overwhelming at times. Our family struggled to find a balance between letting people journey with us and leaving Dana enough energy to be with the kids and me. After all, we were the ones that needed her most. All of the people journeying with us, even family, could go home and escape this suffering. But the kids, Dana and I had to sit in our reality - day in and day out. We couldn't escape it and go home to our healthy family. We had to face it. I began to schedule days where we would close the doors, turn off the chaos and focus on our little family. No one was allowed to stop by. We wouldn't answer our phones. We would have pizza and movie nights, all gathered around Dana's bed. The kids would make cots on the floor and have a sleep over with Mom. We wanted to create lasting moments for them. We wanted plenty of time to say goodbye.

Our family counselor guided us through that process and suggested some things we could do together. The counselor specialized not only in childhood grief but grieving before the death of a loved one with a terminal illness. Some of the things we chose to do were tough to swallow and people outside our madness always had opinions about it. Are you sure that's healthy? That sounds morbid, they would say.

But we trusted the Father to lead us. One of the things we did together was decorating the urn that Dana's ashes would be placed in at the gravesite. She wanted to be cremated and have the ashes buried. There were no rules on what the container had to be other than its size. I went to the craft store and found the perfect little wooden box to decorate. We glued a cross on top and wrote messages to Mommy and each other. It was an awesome moment. Questions and conversations arose about Heaven. Where would Mommy be

58

when she left us? The messages from the kids were precious and sad. But once again, it eased us through the pain. The morphine levels Dana was on were intense, but she kept pushing herself. Her speech was slurred, and for some unknown reason, she lost the ability to read and write. We thought this could be a sign that the cancer had spread to her brain. As we were all painting and writing our notes, I couldn't see Dana's side of the box, but it looked like she was doing ok. She sat back to admire her work. A puzzled look crossed her face.

When I asked what was wrong, she said, "This doesn't say anything, does it?"

As I rotated the box to see her side, I was heartbroken. It looked like a preschooler pretending she could write. It was just scribbling and lines. I felt so bad for her. I wanted to lie, to say no, it looked great. But Dana knew. With tears streaming down her face, she broke down in frustration, "I can't even write a simple message to my kids!"

I said, "It's ok. It's ok. I'll fix it. Just tell me what you want it to say."

With the kids looking on, she quickly pulled herself together, "My heart is full. I want it to say, my heart is full."

I painted the whole thing black, erasing her mistake forever. In big pink letters I wrote, My Heart Is Full – Dana.

Her heart was full? How could that be? We had been through hell. Dana was dying in front of me and our kids. How could her heart be full? That is the miraculous part of her journey. Somehow, God, in His mercy, granted her peace. Peace that the kids, and I would be ok. Peace that she would be in eternity with Jesus, and our joy would somehow be complete. In this kind of suffering, only God could grant that. There's no way she could muster that up in her own strength. We were decorating the urn her ashes would be buried in. But her heart was full. That is a testament to a life submitted to the will of God. Joy in the midst of darkness. Comfort the midst of pain.

Dana had such a passion for life. Seeing that passion leave her broke my heart. Her bright blue eyes that once beamed with light were fading. She wanted to leave a legacy and finish everything on her "to do's" list before she passed. She would frantically go over that list and make sure people were there to help her accomplish it. Things like teaching me how to pay the bills, organizing all of our important files, and giving me all of her online passwords so I could access her accounts. She was leaving for the ultimate trip and never coming back. Everything had to be in place, so we could succeed without her. But in all her striving to live and accomplish that list, the things of earth were "growing strangely dim." As much as it saddened her to let go, her heart was longing for more than this life could give. She was longing for eternity.

Chapter 8

LONGING FOR ETERNITY

Whom have I in heaven but you?
And there is nothing on earth that I desire besides you.
Psalm 73:25 (ESV)

A faithful group of ladies came to the little blue house for a bible study with Dana once a week. They would read together about Heaven and what eternity might look like. Dana would light up and marvel at all the things she might see while she cried and wrestled with all she was losing. As she felt her time drawing near, her outlook began to change.

Her heart was torn between the pain of what those of us who were left behind would face, and the joy she felt in knowing that soon, very soon, she would see the face of Christ. Dana would embrace Christ. She would see His nail scared hands. She would hear angels sing as all the creatures of heaven proclaim, "Worthy is the Lamb!" Loved ones who had passed would await her arrival. Cancer would be no more. How could she not long for that? How could she not long for eternity and being face to face with the God of all creation? It lifted her spirit and brought her sadness all at the same time.

She called it, "an eternal perspective." In death, she had an eternal perspective that all of us should have - a revelation that this life is frail and temporary. Dana learned that in truth, we are all dying. This life on earth is not our true existence. We have a very specific mission, ordained by our creator. We can trust Him and rest in that. If we are submitted to the Father, nothing can stop His plans for us. Our life is not our own. For those who are in Christ, an eternal glory awaits us that we cannot conceive. When death stared Dana in the face for fifteen months, she realized how short this life really is. She began to see a big picture that was there all along. She just wasn't ready to acknowledge it. Life on this earth is not our end. We are here on mission to spread the gospel. We live in a fallen, broken world and are surrounded with that harsh reality. But we can choose to glorify God.

We can rest in His grace even when we face the darkest of circumstances. Dana's heart was full. Even though her life on earth was ending at thirty-seven. She had lived for the glory of Christ. Eternity was near.

Through the center where Dana was treated, we met an amazing hospice nurse, Matt. His wife had terminal cancer as well, so he and I would sit and talk at the hospital while the girls got their chemo. He promised Dana he would be by her side in the end. He said that he would make sure she was never in pain. Once we stopped treatments, Dana and I realized it was time to call Matt.

"Are we sure he's the right one?" Dana asked me in fear.

"Yes Sweetie, I really believe God brought him to us. His own wife is fighting for her life. No one could understand what we are going through better than him. I just hope he can do it with all they are going through." I replied.

We called Matt. He graciously agreed to see Dana through to the end, just as he promised. At first, Matt would come by twice a week and just check in on Dana. He would check her vitals and ask how she was feeling.

She would always ask him one question," How much time do I have?"

We dreaded the answer. It was surreal just trying to understand that timeline. When it would happen? How would it happen? Early on it was hard to say, but as the cancer grew and her symptoms increased, Matt could narrow it down. First it was three or four weeks, then two weeks, then any day now. Time was running out. Eternity was in sight. The pain grew more and more intense. That meant more drugs. Doses were doubled at times. Still Dana would cry out in pain in the middle of the night. Remember, God told me it would get "ugly" before she passed.

Dana could barely walk or talk. Because she was so determined to get things done, caring for her grew challenging. She had that list. She was so close to finishing it. She just couldn't rest until the list was done. The problem was that she slept so much, she never knew what time of day it was. She would wake up in the middle of the night and try to get out of bed.

I was afraid she was going to be hallucinating and fall down the stairs while I slept. I would sleep with my hand on her, so if she moved it would wake me up. Dana was such a busy woman most of her adult life. She was sure there was someone she needed to call, or some kind of task that just had to be done this instant. But she couldn't be the taskmaster she once was. And I couldn't let her hurt herself trying.

It became clear that as the meds increased, I was going to lose the ability to communicate with her. Matt explained the goal was to keep her comfortable and take away as much pain as possible. There were terrifying scenarios that could play out to take Dana's life. I just kept praying it would be peaceful. Matt tried to prepare me for the worst as I prayed for the best. She had fought so hard and touched so many lives in her suffering. I just had to believe that the Father would grant her an easy passing. I asked Him to bring her into eternity with grace and peace. When the pain became more than she could bare, hospice decided to basically put her in a drug-induced coma. It was the only way Matt could keep his promise to keep Dana from tremendous pain. Matt had to set a date for the coma to start, so that she could say her goodbyes. But before he could that, Dana had one final project to cross off her list. Her funeral.

As I said earlier, Dana was determined to plan her own funeral. During her life, she was the ultimate planner. Every "T" was crossed, every "i" dotted. Her funeral would be no exception. Despite the unconscious state the meds put her in, we picked a day to go to the funeral home, of course, the one we drove by every day, the pretty one that brought her peace. Some precious friends agreed to go with us to help in the planning and caring for Dana. It looked like we were going to be able to pull this off. But, when we arrived, we were met with the dilemma that the appointment we thought was set for us was never made. I pleaded with the funeral home to find someone to help us. This poor woman just wanted to plan her own funeral, and her days were numbered. The staff sprang into action, but every funeral planner was booked solid.

As they scrambled to help us, the manager said, "Let's see if Amy can help you."

Amy was not usually involved in near death cases. It was something she did occasionally, but she generally dealt with healthy people's funerals that wanted to plan ahead. Although we weren't her normal case, they called her out of an appointment. After hearing our situation, she agreed to help us out.

Amy was beautiful and gracious. She sat with Dana, the two ladies with us, and me for several hours. We painstakingly planned every detail. We planned a dove release, a balloon release and even designed the headstone. Dana had thought this all out. She wanted the kids to have something memorable at the ceremony. She wanted to be cremated but wanted her ashes buried at a gravesite, so we would have somewhere to visit. She spent that day humped over in a wheelchair. I had to regularly wake her when she would pass out mid-sentence. She was determined to look through every detail herself. As Dana faded in and out of consciousness, Amy patiently waited. I could tell she was holding back tears, but she kept them in and stayed with us.

After several hours, I brought the kids in to see Mom and meet Amy. They wanted to go to the field and pick out the gravesite where Mommy would be buried. This was another one of those things that sounded morbid to everyone else. But to us, it was all a part of our grieving, together, as a family. We took a drive out to the available area where new gravesites were placed. Zachary jumped out of the van, determined to find the spot where Mommy would be placed.

When we got to the field, Zachary ran ahead to a spot he found and said, "It's right here, Daddy."

"It doesn't look like there are any plots there, Buddy." I replied.

It was a field full of headstones. But as Amy walked over to Zach, she discovered there was a plot left in the middle of the field where everything else was taken.

"It looks like this one was left open just for Mommy." Amy said.

It was amazing to see Zach's reaction when he was right. There was a spot there for his mommy. I was so thankful for the strength God had granted him to withstand these circumstances.

Dana wanted to do a little ceremony at the site where she would be placed. There she would give the kids their first trinket from the series she had planned for them with their videos. We all sat down in a circle as she told them about her plan to always be there for them through the videos. As we said a prayer and finished up, Dana began to vomit. It was so frustrating for her. Every outing or sweet moment was always followed by some dramatic cancer issue. It was just how it went for us then. Despite the trials, it was still such a tender time for our family to share. We were somehow forever linked to Amy in it all as well. As I looked off to the side of the road, I could see Amy wiping away tears. She saw it all and gently guided our little family through that tough day. When our family pulled away in the truck, Amy hugged Dana. She told Dana what an inspiration she was to her that day. Amy spoke of how Dana changed her life and said she would never forget the strength and love our family showed her. That was the last time Amy would see Dana.

After the funeral was planned, Dana and I were left with the gut-wrenching task of choosing the day Dana would go to sleep and begin her journey to see Jesus. We opened our doors to a flood of close friends and family who needed to come to say their final goodbyes. There were many tears and much laughter as Dana would comfort those who came to comfort her. That was who Dana was. On the last day, Zach, Zoe and I sat on the bed as she hugged them and said Mommy was going to go to sleep now. She told them that Mommy would still be able to hear them, but that she couldn't respond. She pleaded with them to talk to her while she slept. They wept and held Dana tight for one last time.

Even in the daze from all the meds, she was still focused on her list. She left videos for people and tried to think of anything she may have forgotten to do. All I could do was assure the woman I had loved for nineteen years that it was ok. We were going to be ok. Her list was done. She did it all. Every video for the kids was recorded and in a safe place. It was ok to stop fighting. It was ok to rest and wait for her turn to go home to glory. "Stop fighting, Sweetie, just rest." I would plead. I couldn't bear to watch her suffer any longer. I couldn't bear to have her hurt herself trying to accomplish her list. I think in the end, she was simply torn. She was longing for eternity, but just couldn't let go of this life.

Finally, she couldn't hold on any longer. The moment came when she said she was ready for Matt began to administer the drugs. He asked that we all leave the room for a while to give her some silence. Once she was asleep, Matt went home. He gave me a list of things to watch for and instructions on how to continue giving her meds through the night.

For almost nineteen years, I had laid next to this woman. But now, I was counting the nights until she would no longer be there. I stayed up all night and watched her sleep as her breathing became more and more intense.

At 5:00am I called Matt, "I needed help!"

He rushed to the little blue house and took over for me. He said Dana was progressing quicker than he thought she would.

Matt said, "Nate, call Dana's family over in case this is the day."

As family and friends hung out downstairs, I sat with her and Matt in silence.

She woke up once and said, "Where am I? I want to go back to my brother! Send me back to my brother."

Matt asked where her brother was. I explained to him that she didn't have one. After talking with her parents, we realized that her mother had a miscarriage in the past. We had heard stories of people passing to and from eternity in their final moments. Could she have seen this brother that passed away in a miscarriage?

That was an awesome moment to ponder, but shortly after, her condition began to change. Matt advised me to go downstairs and give him a bit of time with her. Throughout the day she slept so peacefully. Matt did as he promised. He stayed by her side and made sure she felt no pain. But there seemed to be a shift in her condition now. Her breathing was getting very loud and intense. I now know that doctors refer to this as the *death rattle*.

Matt pleaded with me to leave saying, "Nate, you don't want to see this. Please just leave for a bit. I'll let you know when it's safe to come back in."

I just felt so helpless. I was by her side this entire battle. There was no way I could leave her now. But what I was seeing, and hearing was really shocking. I couldn't do it. I reluctantly went downstairs and pleaded with the

Lord to take her peacefully. Mike, the pastor at Joyce Meyer Ministries later comforted me about that moment because it really ate at my soul. I couldn't be there. I couldn't stand to watch it. But his words really meant the world to me.

He said, "Nate, you held her hand and led her through this entire journey, but you were done. It was time for Jesus to take her hand and lead her where you couldn't go."

It was true. She was passing into the hands of God. My covenant with her was ending. She was going where I could not lead her.

We all waited patiently downstairs. The kids were playing, people were talking and reliving all the joy Dana had brought them. It was a celebration of a life well lived. We could celebrate knowing where she was going. She wasn't really dying that day. She was just being released from that cancer riddled body that held her down. She was running into the arms of Jesus for eternity. As we talked and relived moments, Matt came downstairs.

With a heavy sigh said, "It's time."

I'll never forget that walk up those stairs. My legs were suddenly heavy, like they were full of lead. I was about to say goodbye to my wife of nineteen years, my friend and partner in life.

As her family made a circle around her bed, I lay next to her and held her hand. Tears streaming down our faces, we prayed and waited for Matt to announce her passing.

As I lay there, I found myself praying over and over, "Lord take my sister into Your hands. Lord take my sister into Your hands."

I caught on after a few minutes and thought how strange that was. I suddenly had the deep revelation that all this time, she was more than my wife; she was my sister in Christ. The Father had allowed me to journey with her in this life, but it was temporary. As much as I loved her and desperately wanted to take care of her, she was the Father's daughter. He would care for her in eternity. He would care for me and the kids.

As we continued to pray, I held her hand tight. Matt laid a stethoscope on her chest and gently said, "She's gone."

I instantly burst into sobbing. It was like a flood of emotion as well as simple relief hit me all at once. She was gone. But she wasn't in pain. The cancer was no more. She was healed. She had truly just slipped into eternity. I could only imagine what she was seeing there. All the grief and suffering of this world no longer bound her. She was truly free. We could rest in knowing that she would suffer no more. Jesus would hold her now.

I just sat and looked at her face for a while knowing this was the last time I could. My wife of almost 19 years was gone. I didn't know how to leave. How could I walk away from this moment? I couldn't go with her, but how could I face the world without her? I was truly alone for the first time in my adult life. There were two little kids downstairs I now had to lead through a life without their mother.

I finally gathered myself and headed down the stairs to face a new life without Dana, as a single dad. There were lots of hugs and sobbing as we were all in shock. It just seemed so surreal, like we were in this terrible dream sequence from a movie. I walked outside to catch my breath and look for the kids. We didn't think they should see that final moment, so a friend had taken Zoe out to get her nails done. My nephews were supposed to be keeping Zach busy. But where was Zachary? I wanted to gently tell him Dana was gone, but I couldn't find him. There were people all over the little blue house, so I was frantically running around asking where he was. Surely, he did not sneak upstairs to see Dana. Matt was in the middle of cleaning her up but had left the room. There are things that happen after a death that Zach should not see. I sprinted up the stairs and swung the door open. There he was, kneeling at the foot of the bed and ever so gently weeping. It was the saddest thing I could ever imagine.

I knelt beside him and said, "I am so sorry Buddy. I am so sorry.

Why are you up here? You shouldn't see this, Buddy."

He said, "I just wanted to say goodbye."

He hugged me tighter than he ever has. I couldn't imagine what his little heart was feeling. I so desperately wanted to take it away from him. But there was nothing I could do. This was his story. I had the honor of being there in it with him. He was eight years old and his mommy was gone.

PRECIOUS PEACE

By Nate Edmonds and Matt Armstrong
(From the More than All the Glories Worship Project)

There is joy in the darkness, comfort in the pain
There is beauty in the longing, Your word will sustain
I can trust in the promise, Your ways are always true
In the depth of the valley, Your faithfulness will prove

Precious peace, precious peace, let it wash over me
Let my soul sing again, it is well
Precious peace, precious peace, Jesus wash over me
Let me soul sing again, it is well, it is well

There is hope for a future brighter than the past
There is strength for tomorrow, Your love will holdfast
I will trust in the promise, Your ways are always true
In the depth of the valley, Your faithfulness will prove

Precious peace, precious peace, let it wash over me
Let my soul sing again, it is well
Precious peace, precious peace, Jesus wash over me
Let me soul sing again, it is well, it is well

It is well, with my soul
It is well, with my soul
It is well, it is well with my soul

Chapter 9

PRECIOUS PEACE

And the peace of God, which surpasses all understanding,
will guard your hearts and your minds in Christ Jesus.
Philippians 4:7 (ESV)

When I looked ahead to what life would be like after Dana's death, one of my biggest fears was the night of her passing. I couldn't think of a lonelier feeling than that first night, after nineteen years of marriage, going to bed alone. The deafening silence of a room we had once shared, now vacant and left with the empty bed she had suffered in for so long. How could I possibly sleep there? Could I ever stand to be in that room again? What terror and grief would haunt me that dreadful night? But I climbed those stairs once again. Those stairs I had raced up and down all day, every day, for fifteen months, being a twenty-four-hour nurse. Those stairs I climbed earlier that day to hold her hand as she slipped away to eternity. As I climbed the stairs, this amazing and precious peace settled into my heart. It wasn't dreadful at all. In fact, it was actually quite serene. The silence wasn't deafening. It was like a cool breeze washing over my soul. The empty bed was like an empty tomb, a sign that she had risen. She wasn't dead. She was alive in eternity, more alive than she had ever been. I could finally rest. The battle was over. The cancer was gone. I didn't have to carry the weight of it all any longer. Victory was ours in Christ, even in death. We always said she was healed either way - either in eternity or here on earth. Either way, she won. Death has no sting when you have an eternal perspective.

I slept peacefully, so peacefully. I was amazed. In fact, this precious peace just settled into the little blue house. The next day Pastor Marc came by to go over the funeral arrangements.

"Wow Nate, do you feel that? he asked. It's incredible how peaceful it is here."

I said, "Yes I do. I've been resting in it all day."

It was a sweet gift from the Lord after all we'd been through. That precious peace would follow us all through the next couple of days as the final preparations were made. Our family went to the funeral home for a private open casket ceremony before the cremation.

I cleared the room, so the kids and I could have our last moment with Dana. Through our counseling we had been given four little glass hearts. They were to keep in our pockets for the future. Every time we missed Mommy, we could rub those hearts and remember all the good things about her. As I asked the Father how to make this moment special, He gave me an idea. We placed all four of our little glass hearts on Dana's heart and Zach, Zoe and I prayed. We committed Mommy's spirit to the Lord. We pleaded for strength for us all. We prayed for our future and asked the Father to lead us into healing and something amazing for His glory. Then we took our heart's back and placed them in our pockets. We left Mommy's glass heart laying on her chest. She was at peace, and so were we. A precious peace was ours.

Over a thousand people came to pay their respects at the wake. I stood at the front of the church for four hours as a line formed around the building. People wanted to celebrate Dana's life. It was incredible to see how she had affected so many lives. How her strength and unflinching love for God had drawn people to Christ. One by one, they walked up and showed us an outpouring of love. At the end of that night, I was completely exhausted. But I had to push through for one more tough day.

The next day we had a celebration. Hundreds of people gathered at Matthias' Church to honor the God that gave Dana life. The stage was covered with flowers and pictures. Dana's ashes were placed in the urn we decorated as a family and sat on a table for everyone to see. Before Dana passed, she asked me to speak and sing at her funeral. At first, I said there was no way I could keep it together through that. But God quickly spoke through some faithful brothers that encouraged me to do it. God granted me strength. Pastor Marc and I both spoke. I led us all in worship, singing the songs that were closest to our hearts in the battle. The songs Dana and I sang in the night when all we could do was whisper, everyone now sang with the congregation of friends and family that gathered as well as the hosts of Heaven. We sang with a loud voice and celebrated all that the Lord had done in Dana's life. At Dana's request, Brandon, the Worship Pastor at Matthias' Lot, sang the old hymn "It Is Well." It was a precious day I will cherish forever. It was well with our souls. That precious peace continued to wash over us.

During Dana's battle, a company that prints tee shirts for charity, started a bit of a revolution. They sold hundreds of shirts with the words from scripture *Take Heart* printed on them to raise money for our family. Per Dana's wishes, everyone wore jeans to the celebration and sported their *Take Heart* tee shirts. There was a sea of them throughout the church. It was so amazing to see all the love and support our family had. As we wrapped up the service and said the final prayer with the kids, I felt a tug on my shirt. It was Zach.

He said, "Daddy, I want to play drums."

I was surprised and didn't quite know what to say. I didn't want to deny him that, but it felt a little inappropriate. Pastor Marc had heard him.

We looked at each other, shrugged our shoulders and said, sure, why not?

Zach got on the drums and played his little heart out for his mommy and all who loved her. He was like the little drummer boy in the Christmas Carole. He didn't have much else to bring, but he could play the drums. He played until the congregation began to cheer. It was out of the ordinary but fitting to our journey. Dana would have been so proud of her little man and his strength that day. He worshiped through his pain and ushered in that precious peace.

After the service, everyone got in their cars. There was a massive procession to the gravesite where Dana's ashes would be buried. We had a beautiful service, just as Dana planned, with a dove release and balloon release for the kids. We wrote messages on the balloons to Mommy. The kids and I watched the doves move in perfect sequence as they flew off into the sun, just like Dana's spirit.

When all the activities were done, the kids and I walked over to the grave. We put the sweet urn we had decorated with Mommy into the ground and tossed a handful of dirt on top. It was done. This was the end of a painful, bittersweet chapter of our lives. The grave would be covered with a bronze plate that was engraved with six simple words, for His glory, by His grace.

Those words still summed it all up. Every trial. Every storm we faced. Every moment of victory and triumph, all accomplished by His grace alone, for His glory alone. We were poured out an offering, for His majesty. He would make our ruins His masterpiece. We would turn and face a new adventure, just the three of us now. We would have to trust the Father for that same irresistible grace to carry us through.

I wanted to lighten the load for the kids that day. We had seen so much. Now we were starting this new adventure together. My sister, Shelly and I loaded them into the new truck and went to the toy store. We bought all kinds of stuff. I even bought myself some toys. We went home to all our family gathered at the little blue house. It was a peaceful night. Our incredible church family had brought us a sea of food and drinks. My entire family was there. My parents, all four sisters, their spouses and kids, all in the little blue house. It was quite a night. We lit a bonfire and sat around just relaxing and taking in all that we'd been through. That sting and weight of watching Dana suffer was gone. This precious peace just continued to comfort us. It was so cleansing. It healed our souls.

As my family packed up and headed home over the next couple of days a reality set in that I knew was coming. It was just going to be the three of us now. All the activity and buzz of battling the cancer as well as all the visitors were gone. It was a very lonely feeling. We would need this peace and grace now more than ever. I was a single dad with two grieving kids. I would have to navigate those waters alone, without my best friend and helpmate. It was a sobering thought, but one I had already visited in my mind and heart for many months now.

I felt the strength of the Lord rising up in me as well as this peace that God had a plan. It was definitely tough at first. No more meals coming at night. All the chores, errands, and meal preparation were up to me. School had started a few weeks before Dana passed. Now, I would have to do the homework and reading alone with the kids. But we were doing it, just the three of us.

Moments of grief were a regular and welcomed thing, though very mild and short lived. We were settling into this new, peaceful life. A few weeks later it was time to go get Rufus! He was the dog we had picked out with Dana. We had made several trips to visit him after he was born, but now it was time for him to move in with us. I had also bought another fluffy Goldendoodle a few weeks before thinking Rufus needed a friend. Max and Rufus McGee were their names.

All the teachers and staff at the school thought I had lost my mind when I walked up with these two giant puppies on a leash. They said, I was a brave man and couldn't believe I was taking all that on. But it was honestly so much fun. My family was alive and doing this together. It was well with our souls. The moments of grief were hedged in on all sides with moments of peace and joy. We knew something great was around the corner. Just like God restored double what Job had lost in the Bible, He was going to restore us as well.

The kids needed to see my strength in Christ and know I was following through with the plan - *a truck, a dog (or two), and a trip*. We had a sure foundation to stand on. Everything was ok. All we needed now was a trip. I threw out several options, but the kids really wanted to bring the dogs. As frightening as that was for me, I thought it was a good idea. I mean why not? Two dogs and two kids with a single dad on a road trip. How tough could it be?

Thanksgiving was approaching so we decided to drive to New York to see Aunt Shelly and all our festive Italian New York family. They were full of laughter and activity. There was always tons of amazing food. It would be a Thanksgiving we would never forget. We had made that trip with Dana once. I remembered a hotel she found at the half way point where there was a waterpark. I called, and they accepted pets. It was perfect. Mommy was still looking after us.

We loaded up the truck with all the pillows, toys, electronics, movies, suitcases and of course Max and Rufus. We hit the road. Being a single dad on a trip felt daunting at first, but so necessary to our healing. We left in the early morning. As the sun came up, I could see their two little heads in my review mirror - each with a dog in their lap. What was going on in their hearts, I'll never know. Could I be enough for them? I was worried that I was taking on too much. I feared I would just stress out at some point. But it never came to that. It was peaceful and fun.

Finally reaching our half way point, we put the dogs in cages and hit the waterpark. The kids were laughing and playing. We ordered pizza and sat around the pool for several hours. Dana would be proud of us. She was smiling on us. The kids having fun was always her first priority. At one-point, Zachary busted his lip wide open on a waterslide. Blood was everywhere. This was a moment when Mommy would have stepped in and comforted him. But I handled it. I was his comforter now. We were making the most of every moment. We were proving to ourselves and everyone else that we had this. We could do this because God was with us. He had a plan. We just knew it. This precious peace would guide us, so we could live again. Dana would be proud of us.

Arriving in New York for Thanksgiving, my Italian side of the family got into hospitality mode. There was wine, meatballs and turkey for days. It was relaxing and fun despite the fact that my sister had two dogs and a cat as well.

83

If you're counting, that's four dogs and a cat. Every morning we'd hit the streets with leashes and mutts in hand for daily walks. We laughed and laughed some more. It breathed the life into us we so desperately needed. We stuck to the plan. It was all working together for our good. But what came next was quite a surprise.

We didn't see it coming and certainly didn't plan on it. But God did. He was about to lead us into a whole new adventure.

Chapter 10

A NEW ADVENTURE

The heart of man plans his way,
but the Lord establishes his steps.
Proverbs 16:9 (ESV)

As the weeks went by after Dana passed, there were some details I had to talk over with Amy, the funeral planner, regarding the headstone and when the final engraved piece would be installed. She was always professional with me, calling me Mr. Edmonds. Amy was so kind to our family. She wanted to follow our story and friended us online. I had never looked her up there until one day when she popped up in my news feed looking for a new church. She said in a post that she was going through a tough season and needed a fresh start. I felt compelled to help her. Our family had a meaningful connection with her the day we planned Dana's funeral. Hearing that she was going through a rough time in her life broke my heart. I responded to her post and invited her to our church. She said she'd be there.

The service she attended happened to be on a week when I was leading worship. I always sat in the same place, in the back of the church. When I came off the platform, I went to my usual spot and saw Amy there. The church was packed and one of the only seats in the house was next to Amy. I asked her if it was taken. Of course, she let me sit there. We said, hi.

I said, "I'm glad you came."

We talked a bit afterwards, and that was pretty much it.

Over the next few weeks, I would see Amy at church. We'd say, hello. Sometimes we'd have a quick talk or sometimes just wave from across the church. I always felt like I needed to help her somehow, but I didn't know what that meant or what I was really feeling. We would text once in a while. We'd see how the other was doing, or say it was nice to see you at church again, but never any real conversation.

While I was in New York, I couldn't get Amy off my mind. She was so stunning. I felt drawn to her kind spirit.

I was joking with my sister all Thanksgiving week that Amy was so beautiful and her name, Amy Sommerville; the prettiest name I had ever heard.

It became a running joke that week. "Amy Sommerville, the prettiest name of all," I would say.

I was a happily married man for nineteen years. I didn't know what in the world I was feeling. Did I have a crush on this woman? I would think to myself.... what is wrong with me? Why can't I stop thinking about her? It felt so foreign to me, but it was exhilarating. I had thought my plan was not to even consider dating for at least a year, but I just felt like my heart was ready.

I was tired of grief and sorrow. I had honestly gotten on a few dating sites just out of sheer curiosity to see what was out there for a man my age. Through the counseling we had as a family during Dana's illness, the kids and I had done so much grieving up front with Dana. The counseling and time in payer, allowed me to start letting my heart feel the pain of losing her a year before she was gone. Dana said over and over, that I would remarry quickly, and she blessed it.

She even warned her friends about it saying, "Please don't hate her. I want you to accept her and love her."

Could this be what she was talking about?

Two days before Thanksgiving, my sister, the kids and I were out shopping. The kids were really acting up.

My sister said, "Nate, why don't you take a break for a second and go get some coffee. I have the kids."

Sipping my coffee while aimlessly walking the aisles of the store, all I could think about was Amy. I began to pray and asked the Father what in the world I should do.

I prayed, "Should I text her or something? What am I feeling? Are the kids and I ready for this? "

I felt like I should go for it. I felt like God had given me a green light, and I was going for it! I grabbed my phone and sent the text that started it all.

I said, "So…. you're a bit of a puzzle to me Miss Sommerville. Tell me something about you I don't know."

Then the floodgates were opened. We started texting like crazy. I would send a text and anxiously await her response. I would grab my sister and say, "She responded!"

We would sit and read it together. I needed advice! I didn't know how dating worked these days. What should I say? It was so fun, and I felt alive. I didn't know where this could lead, but I knew there was something very special about this woman. I had to find out more.

By the end of the week, we were texting every day and talking on the phone. I couldn't wait to get home because I wanted to see her. Our talks weren't shallow or flirtatious. We talked about real stuff. She was so genuine. She was honest about her past. The years of abuse she had suffered. She owned up to her choices in life and wanted to stop the patterns of brokenness she was in.

The day the kids, Dana and I met Amy, she was truly inspired by the weight of our situation and the strength that God had given us as a family. She saw what she wanted for her own life and began to ask God to grant her that kind of strength. She wanted a relationship with Christ at the center. She was a single mom with three kids - Owen, Mason and Heidi. God needed to make some major changes in her life and set her on a path of healing. Now, here we were, just a few months after meeting, texting like crazy and having these candid talks. Could this be the answer to her prayers, mine, and honestly... Dana's?

The more we talked the more drawn to her I became. I just wanted to know her. So, we set a "date". I would see her face to face as soon as I got home from New York. We would text on every stop, the entire ride home. We counted the hours until we could see each other face to face. Our date was set for a Thursday, but I couldn't wait that long and found a way to push it to Monday. But on Sunday, I got a little excited as I passed by her work. It was right by our house, so I sent a text to see if the kids and I could swing by and say, hello. She was all for it. Zach and Zoe heard some of my sister and I talking about Amy. They were so open to me dating.

They talked about it all the time and made fun of me saying, "Daddy's gonna have a girlfriend ooh, ah. Daddy's in love"

Of course, little Zoe couldn't contain her excitement. As soon as we were face to face with Amy, she says with her little girl voice...

"If my daddy mawwies you, and yewa thwee kids, we awe gonna need a biggow caw."

That's Zoe speak for *"IF MY DADDY MARRIES YOU, AND YOUR THREE KIDS, WE ARE GONNA NEED A BIGGER CAR!"*

Oh my gosh! I was horrified! I was bright red faced and had no idea how to fix what just happened.

I quickly put my hand on Zoe's mouth and said, "We have not talked about marrying you! I don't know where she got that!"

But Amy just grabbed Zoe, smiled and very smoothly said, "No we won't, I have a big SUV right outside in the parking lot that will fit us all."

Then she grinned and looked at me to see my response. I was stunned and thinking, wow, that just happened. We were all feeling the same things. Amy and I hadn't even had our first date yet, but we could feel what was happening. It felt like the Father was guiding us all. Deep inside, we all knew where we were headed.

Monday finally came, and it was time for our first date! While I was in New York, I saw Amy's post online that she really wanted a certain cookbook she used to have. She said she had lost it in a move from Holland to The States. It meant a lot to her. God gave me the idea to hunt one down for her. I found one, had it gift-wrapped, and overnighted to my house. I couldn't wait to give it to her. As God would have it, our first date started with some chaos. It was like He was preparing us for some real-life adventure. Amy popped her tire. Her car was stuck on the side of the road. I picked her up there and put her tire in the back of my truck to have it replaced for her.

It was pretty romantic. A sign that I would always be there for her. I wanted to help her in every way I could. When we got the tire situation all figured out, we got in my truck to finally start our date.

I looked in the back seat and said, "Hmm, what's this huge package back here?"

I grabbed the gift and set it in her lap. She smiled, "What's this?"

I said, "Just something small for you to start our date. Nothing big."

When she opened the gift bag she looked so stunned. "How did you know? I've been missing this for years."

"I saw your post."

She started to cry. "How sweet. No one has ever done anything like this for me before."

We were off to a great start!

I gave her a couple of options for food. She picked my favorite Thai restaurant. We got past the casual talks and really started to connect over lunch. After that, I had a plan to take her to Main Street. Sitting in a little coffee house, I couldn't believe our conversation. We sat close, staring into each other's eyes and talking for five hours straight. Amy shared more of her story with me. She shared the abuse she had suffered as a child and how it led her to some of the choices she had made as an adult. We shared our biggest successes and failures. We talked about our kids, her ten years in Europe, and why she was fluent in Dutch. We talked about what we wanted in a relationship. We were in sync on so many levels. Her beauty, inside and out, was enchanting. I just wanted to look at her face and hear her heart.

I had asked the Father for a lot of criteria I desired in a new spouse. Mostly, that she would love Jesus, and be good to my little ones. But selfishly, I had this one small request. I asked Him if she could have a beautiful face. I wanted to be able to gaze at her and forget about everything I had been through. I wanted to be madly in love with her. Here I was thinking, Amy's it, man. She's breathtaking. Her tender heart blessed me so much. I hung on every word she said. The life she had lived both broke my heart and inspired me. She was so strong. God had done a work in her.

Over the next week, things just got more and more intense. Amy and I introduced all the kids to each other. We hung out together every chance we got. The kids, the dogs, everyone. The kids quickly warmed up to each other. They were playing and sitting on the couch together right away. We couldn't believe all the intense emotion and compassion we suddenly developed. We knew we loved each other. One night over the phone Amy and I were having a long talk. It was past midnight. She was desperately trying to tell me how she felt about me without saying those three scary words, and I knew it. I pushed a little further.

I said, "Amy Sommerville, you love me, don't you?"

Her response was, "Yep, Yep, I do!"

It was finally out. God had done something extraordinary in us that we could not explain. We felt like we had known each other our whole lives, but it had only been a week! I'm not kidding, by the end of that week we looked back and would swear it was a month. It felt like such a long time. It felt like we were sucked into some kind of time warp.

Over the course of the next few weeks, we were blown away by all that the Father did in the kids and us.

We were together every night we could be. The kids laughed and played. The dogs barked and chased each other. We even went grocery shopping together one Saturday. We wanted to see what it would be like to be a family. The store had little carts for the kids. Amy, Zoe and Heidi all went one way with their carts and a list. Owen, Zach, Mason, and me all went another way with our carts. I'll never forget the look on Amy's face as we split up to hit the shopping aisles.

I looked at her and said, "We've got this, Baby. We've got this."

And we did. We packed up the big black SUV with kids and groceries, and got it done, like families do. We cooked meals, watched movies, and hung out every day. Things were moving so fast. We felt like we couldn't stop it. We wanted to honor God with our relationship. We didn't want to appear unwise or love struck. Why couldn't we just slow down and pace ourselves? I was seeking all kinds of counsel from my spiritual leaders and brothers in Christ. I was so afraid I was going to make a wrong move. I would wake up every day at 4:30am and pray and journal until 5:30 when Amy would call me. We'd pray together, then she'd give me her worship song for the day. It was a precious time. Something very beautiful was happening that was beyond our control. As I prayed and sought counsel, most everyone felt the same way. Conventional wisdom would say, slow down and pace yourselves. But sometimes, God does unconventional things. We had mentioned marriage several times! How could this be? Amy swore she would never marry again, and now this?

In truth, there is no biblical mandate for how long you should date before you marry, or how long you should wait to marry after the death of a spouse. I would never recommend anyone attempt what we were doing. But this felt like God on every level. Our kids were all onboard and excited for us to all be together. They wanted us to get married, so we could live in the same house. We wanted to build a new life for us all to enjoy. Me, Amy, five kids and three dogs. We couldn't do that unless we were married. We needed each other. We were two single parents trying to do everything on our own. We were so in love that we couldn't stand it. We hated being living in two separate houses.

Amy was so moved by our family the day we met, and the love God had granted us. She had been praying for a man that would respect and value her. She wanted a spiritual leader. A man who would put God first in his life with her. She wanted to stop living in patterns she was repeating from her past and do things God's way. She didn't realize it until now, but what she was seeking was a Godly relationship. If the Father would let me, grant me this one prayer, I wanted to rescue her. I wanted to rescue her from the patterns she was stuck in relationally. I wanted to sweep her off her feet and truly be a

93

Godly man for her. I wanted a covenant with her that would cover all of her past. We could start a new, Christ centered life together. I loved her deeply. I couldn't explain it. I loved how she was with my kids. She worked with grieving people a lot and understood what we were dealing with.

Amy and Zoe were precious together. The first time we were all in church, Zoe climbed up in her arms and put her forehead to Amy's. They began to cry, tears streaming down their face. They sang and worshiped together. It melted my heart. I didn't think about it when we first sat down, but we were in the seats we used to worship in with Dana. Now, in this new season, Amy was there for Zoe. It was like the Father was uniting their hearts and forever linking them in His love.

As I sat and watched them in awe, I also noticed something else happening. Rows of ladies from the church were running out in tears. They were still grieving for Dana. Although I knew God was moving, they couldn't see it. All they could think of was Dana and their loss. It broke my heart. The direction I truly felt the Father was leading my family in was hurting people I loved. But what was I to do, stop the blessing of God for my family? I knew this was the Father and His goodness to us. I knew the pain we had all been through. Zach, Zoe and me with our grief and burdens. Amy, Owen, Mason and Heidi with an incredible story of triumph through struggles. Even those who journeyed close with us could never possibly understand how badly we needed this new love we had found. We wanted to let our heart's mend and breath and live again. From my side, our grieving process started a year before Dana passed. We grieved with her. We were simply in a different place than everyone else. The Father knew we needed a fresh start. From Amy's side, the kids endured a divorce, moved to a different country, and had been apart for a year. There was also a recent separation for Amy that was full of challenges.   The Father knew they needed a stable family to cling to.   We had to embrace what He was doing and trust His goodness for us.   We didn't want to hurt others in the process, but there's no road map for this stuff.   It was going to be a challenge for us all to navigate.

In all honesty, over the next few weeks it became hard for us to be around anyone but our family.   Some people were simply grieving and not ready to journey with us.   But others were vicious.   Judgment came at us from every side.   I knew what we were doing seemed crazy.   But we knew it was the Lord.   I had done nothing but prove my love for God and my family over the past eighteen months.   Yet, there was so much misunderstanding around us, we just didn't know where to turn.   My spiritual leaders were with us and gave us their blessing if we chose to get married. They felt this was the Father's will, but also felt it would definitely be easier if we could wait a year.   But we just felt we couldn't.   We knew what was right for us.   I clung to what I heard the Father speaking to me and a few solid brothers that stood by my side.

One such brother was a dear friend, Troy.   He had started journeying with me in the midst of the cancer storm.   I couldn't believe how our stories collided.   His wife had passed from cancer a few years prior, so he was ahead of me in the battle.   He would talk to me for hours and guide me through twists in the road ahead he had already walked through.   He was a Godsend. As crazy as it sounds, he too married very quickly after his wife passed and faced the same opposition.   Even crazier, both his new wife and Amy were ex-models with a similar past.   It was so amazing that the Father had brought us together to help us both heal.   Troy and his wife Jamie's advice and guidance were priceless to Amy and me.   It gave us strength to face this decision with unflinching faith. It was one more confirmation we needed to press on. God was so faithful to always bring comfort and direction in the storm.

As I prayed one day, I had a vision from the Father. I saw Dana in heaven. She was standing in a beautiful green valley, dressed in a flowing, white summer dress. There were children laughing and playing all around. The air glistened and shimmered. It was like I could see the air.

In a glowing light Dana said, "Oh Nate, why do you worry so much? God is with you. It's ok. When we get here, we are all just children of God. This is the Father. This is good."

Then I heard the Father say, "Run to her. The covenant will cover."

I instantly wrote in my journal, in all caps, *RUN TO HER. THE COVENANT WILL COVER.* It will cover both your pasts. It will cover all of your future. I had this knowing that as long as we were married, God would honor His word. We would have a blessed life. A covenant is literally a contract between God and man. We needed the blessing and promise of God over this relationship. This covenant between Amy and me, and God would protect us. In that moment I realized none of these earthly circumstances or conventional wisdom mattered. God was doing something extraordinary. Sometimes, He chooses to defy conventional wisdom. The covenant of marriage would cover us. It's a beautiful covenant that makes two flesh become one. God would use it to heal us both. The Father was in this.

That day I called all of my spiritual leaders. I asked them to take a deep breath and trust me. I knew it was crazy. I was well aware of all that was at stake. But I had proven throughout this whole journey that I knew the Father's voice. I knew what we had to do. Once again, we went for it. We trusted that the Father was leading us. We were stepping into a new adventure with God.

Chapter 11

I RAN TO HER

*He who finds a wife finds a good thing
and obtains favor from the Lord.*
Proverbs 18:22 (ESV)

It was early December. Christmas was fast approaching. We weren't sure how we were going to pull it off, but we wanted to get married right away. It was exciting and exhilarating. It was unconventional and unexplainable. It was scary and risky. There was more at stake than we could even account for. But Amy and I just knew. We were meant to be. God had granted us a miracle. The Father had brought us to each other in His great love for us. That meant we could trust Him. That meant I needed a ring and a really amazing proposal. Amy said she didn't care what kind of ring it was, as long as it sparkled. I pulled a favor from Dan Meyer to hook me up with a jeweler their family has used for years. They crafted a beautiful custom ring, just for Amy. Of course, it really sparkled. Next step, epic proposal!

A friend of mine, Katie, is a wedding planner in Herman, Missouri. Herman is an old German town set amid gorgeous rolling hills, wineries, and small cafes. I met Katie through Dana's battle. Katie's family runs a foundation for families facing cancer called Shining Hope. I thought of Katie and remembered all the influence she had in that little town, just west of St. Charles. I knew she could pull off something epic with short notice. I made the call. In just a few days, Katie and I had it all figured out. Amy knew I was going to propose because we sat for hours and talked about how we should get married sometime soon. I told her to open up her schedule for a day. I wouldn't tell her why or where we were going, but I needed an entire day of her time. Amy picked a date and Katie made sure every detail was meticulously in place.

Just a week later, the morning came for my big proposal. I was so excited. I got to Amy's house early in the morning. When she came to the door, I was blown away. Amy was breathtaking, and I was about to ask her to be my wife. How did this happen? How could this stunning woman want to be a widower's wife? My nerves were causing a frenzy inside me. I couldn't wait for her to see what I had planned for her. I asked her to come and sit outside with me to talk for a bit. As we sat on the porch, and I fished for a subject to fill the time until Step One of my plan showed up, a huge, all white limousine drove by the house. I guess the driver didn't see the address, so he passed us by.

Amy said, "Hmm, that's strange. Why is there a limo in my subdivision?"

I couldn't hold it in. I just smiled really big.

Amy said, "No, did you do that for us?"

I said, "Surprise! This is one of the many things I have in store for you today."

She was so excited. She kept saying, "You didn't have to do all this."

But I couldn't help myself. Amy had been through so many hardships and struggles in her life. I wanted to be good to her, extraordinarily good to her. I wanted to rescue her, sweep her off her feet. I felt as if the Father had commissioned me to. I felt the Father wanted to show His goodness and love for her, through me. I was so honored to be chosen for this mission. Amy was a precious gift, a daughter of the King that was about to be in my charge and care.

We hopped in the limo and headed out for long drive to Herman. We held each other tight and talked the whole way there. Her eyes lit up as she prodded me for information about where we were going. I'm terrible at keeping surprises a secret. I was dying to tell her everything. I may have leaked a few small details under the pressure, but not much. We drove down some beautiful windy roads and finally pulled up to our first destination. It's a huge winery on a hilltop, overlooking rolling hills and the small town below. She didn't know it, but the staff had shut the whole place down. It was just the two of us. We tasted some wines then I asked her if she'd like a tour. She said yes, not knowing it was all part of the plan.

The staff led us down into the cellar where there were vintage wine barrels and decades of history. Some of the barrels were ten-foot-tall and a hundred years old. The cellar was like nothing I had seen. As we rounded the first few corners, we came upon a dozen pink roses, her favorite of course. There was a small pink note attached that read, "From Death to love our journey began."

Amy smiled and said, "I'm starting to think you planned this little tour."

I said, "Of course, I did, Baby. It's all just for you."

We rounded a few more corners. There was a single rose with another note that read… "My heart joined to yours with a bind that can withstand."

Next stop, another rose and note…. "Anything that life may bring, as long as we are hand in hand." Then there was a narrow staircase leading further into the cellar. As we worked our way down the path, we heard music playing. It was the first worship song Amy had shared with me in our morning prayer time. The lyrics simply said, "Here's my heart Lord, speak what is true." There were candles everywhere with dozens of roses scattered around. Placed on the floor, in a perfect circle in front of a beautiful old wine vat, were still more pink rose pedals.

Kneeling down and picking up the last pink note, she read, "You're my love, my life, my heart is yours forever." A photographer hid in the corner to capture every moment, as I got down on one knee. My heart flooded with emotion and joy as I shared all that I felt for her. I told her how thankful I was that the Father had brought us together. And of course, I asked her to marry me. She said, yes! I stood and embraced her. We danced face to face as our song played out.

So many hardships and life circumstances had led us to this moment. We had dated for less than a month. But here we were in this beautiful setting, committing to marry one another. We wanted a covenant with each other and God. Only the Father, in His goodness, could ordain such love. Only He could sustain it. The covenant would cover.

We were in for quite a ride with five kids and three dogs. But we were so ready to dive in, to go after this life that God had brought to us. Amy prayed for a Godly man. Now I was praying for the strength to be that man for her. I prayed for a Godly woman that would love the kids and me. I prayed for someone who would understand all we had been through.

Oh yes, and I prayed for a beautiful face. Staring at her in this moment, I knew I had found it all.

We jumped into the limo waiting outside and rushed to our next stop. We couldn't have a wedding without a beautiful dress. With Amy's modeling past, trying on beautiful wedding dresses was a must. I wanted her to have an experience she would never forget. My friend Katie also runs a large wedding dress company, so she set up an unbelievable time for Amy. Amy's mother, grandmother and a few friends met us in Katie's storage area where there were thousands of dresses from top designers. They were all lined up on racks, aisle after aisle, Amy hunted for her perfect one.

Then Amy got to try them on. Dress after dress she strutted out to the awe of her friends and family. They let me sneak a peek at a couple they thought wouldn't be "the one".

"The look on your face is priceless, my love," I said.

Wiping away tears, "I've never had someone treat me like this," she replied.

103

She was so beautiful. Beaming in pure white, the bride she was meant to be, the Father's daughter and my love. She was breathtaking. She selected two dresses and ordered them in her size. We didn't know when we'd need them. But a wedding was coming soon.

Next was lunch at another winery and a tour of a few venues where we could possibly have our wedding and reception. We went from place to place dreaming of what our wedding could be like. It was surreal. We asked ourselves how all this was happening so quickly. This was our story. We were living it to the fullest. It just felt like we had been together for years. It was as natural as any other couple planning a wedding. We looked at the cost and size of the venue.

"How much can we afford, Nate?"

"I'll let you know when we are there," I said with a wink. "My question is, who will officiate? Mike or Pastor Marc? I love them both."

"I'll trust you to figure that out, baby. I'm going to focus on the flowers and bridesmaid's dresses."

We wondered how many people would come. Where would we get the cake? You know, normal stuff that engaged couples do after dating less than thirty days. It was so fun. I was so honored to be able to give these things to Amy. I just couldn't stop thinking of ways to be good to her. I wanted to spoil her and make her feel like a princess for the day. The Father had brought me a precious gift in Amy. I was determined to let her know that she was cherished and loved. Not just by me, but by the God of the universe. He saw every hurt and every tragic thing that had been done to her. He had put so much love for her in my heart, I couldn't contain it. After all the stops, we headed home. The drive back was sweet. We stared at her beautiful ring and dreamt of all the things to come.   Where would we vacation with the kids? How would the Father lead us in ministry? Would we make a sixth kid? Life was good.   We were in love.   I had pulled off the epic proposal of her dreams. It was time for our life together to begin.

As the days went on, the onslaught of worries, opinions and attacks against our character continued. We received hateful phone calls and emails, as well as talks from friends and family that were simply concerned. We realized what we were doing seemed crazy.   But why were people questioning our character? I stood by Dana and my children to the bitter end. I served them with all I had. It was the most valiant time of my life as a man. Now, I was being accused of being with Amy before Dana passed. I was called a cult leader. Crazy stuff. And some of it came from people I thought were trusted friends. Our resolve to be married grew. We wanted to run away from it all, build an island for our new family and shut the world out. How could we be together and build this new life without hurting those still grieving? How could we shelter ourselves from the skeptics and critics? We knew what the Father had given us and so desperately wanted everyone to join us in our new adventure. But it just wasn't possible.

Our sphere of counsel grew ever smaller. We relied on a faithful few to continue to journey with us. As we talked and prayed endlessly, it became clear. There would be a time for a big celebration someday. But for now, we needed that covenant to cover us. The Father put a burning desire in us we knew was right. We couldn't have a big wedding at this stage. Who would have come with all the controversy going on? Amy had never had that white dress and chapel moment. I so desperately wanted to give that to her. But this was our lot. The kids were so excited and wanted us all to be together. We wanted to be married. The rest of the world would hopefully come around one day. Time would heal. The wisdom we knew the Father had granted us would be revealed in its season. We had to think of our little gang of crazy kids and follow our hearts. Something extraordinary was happening. We didn't want it to stop. This new adventure was glorious and healing. We decided on a simple wedding.

At a Christmas party with my Aunt Tori and Uncle Dan, my uncle was listening to all Amy and I were facing.

He jokingly said, "Between your cousins and me, there's three ordained ministers here, Nate. Why don't you just go get a marriage license, and we'll get this thing done?"

My Uncle Dan was the one who encouraged me to marry Dana. He told me to get a ring on her finger before I lost her. Now, he was seeing the Lord's hand in this union as well. I looked at Amy. We both had the same thought. Why not? We knew we were meant to be. There was no doubt in our hearts. So why wait? There are times in life when you just know. The spirit of God speaks to your heart and you know.

We called my uncle the next day. "Let's do it! We are holding you to your offer!"

"You mean you want me to marry you guys?"

"Yes! As soon as possible!"

He graciously accepted, and told us he believed in us, no matter what anyone else was saying.

We planned a very impromptu wedding that weekend. We ran out the next day to get our license. We were getting married!

Mind you, this is something I would never recommend to a new couple. Unless…. they knew that they knew it was the Father. Again, conventional wisdom would say wait, make sure. But there was this urgency in us we could not explain. We felt so amazing and alive together.

It was exhilarating to run to this new life. We knew that incredible healing awaited us all through this marriage. It was the boundless love and goodness of the Father to us. He would be our guide. A day after we got our license, we were married.

Amy's oldest boy, Owen, was out of the country with his dad, so we decided we wouldn't have any of the kids there. We knew there would be a time when we could all celebrate together. This was just for us. In fact, we didn't invite anyone.

We were married in my uncle Dan's home. My Aunt Tori and Uncle Dan performed the quaint ceremony in their living room. My parents signed as witnesses. It was a precious day Amy and I will never forget.

Given the grandeur of my proposal, this definitely wasn't what Amy and I wanted our wedding to be. But we knew the Father had a plan. We felt we were being set apart for something great. We needed that covenant, that contract between us and God, quickly. Even though we didn't fully understand why. It was as if this fierce battle was raging all around us. We needed immediate shelter. The assaults against our character were so vile and intense. People were accusing us of horrible things. We were forced to have a humble beginning, but we believed God had an extravagant destiny for our new family.

After the simple wedding we spent the night in a beautiful historic home on Main Street in St. Charles. We held each other close and dreamed of all we could be together. Amy was actually incredibly ill that night with some kind of cold. From day one of this adventure it seemed we would face test after test. Like Amy blowing a tire for the first time in her life, an hour before our date. It was like God was strengthening us for adversity. He continued to build upon that foundation. We were about to take on so much. Five kids, three dogs and what felt like the opinions of the entire world coming at us. But this union had a beauty we couldn't explain. Zach, Zoe, Max, Rufus and I all moved into a new house Amy had purchased a few months before we met. Amy, Owen, Mason and Heidi also had a dog named Gypsy. That makes me, Amy, five kids and three dogs!

We were back in suburbia and in for quite an adventure. There were boxes everywhere as we tried to decide whose household items we would keep. We began construction on the basement, so each kid could have their own room. I also built myself a creative space where I could write this book and the songs that accompany it. It was a time filled with God's glory and grace. Like Zach, Zoe and I, Amy and her kids had been through a lot of hard changes. The Father was healing us all, together, through His love. He placed that love in each one of us for each other. He was working all things together for our good. A blended family, in Christ. But, the bliss of this new love was about to be cut short. God was pushing us to marry quickly and build this new shelter for a reason. We couldn't see it. But there was another storm up ahead.

Chapter 12

ANOTHER STORM ON THE HORIZON

And I say, "Oh, that I had wings like a dove!
I would fly away and be at rest;
yes, I would wander far away;
I would lodge in the wilderness; Selah
I would hurry to find a shelter
from the raging wind and tempest."
Psalm 55:6-8 (ESV)

About a month after Dana's passing, I needed to go back to work. It was time to return to what was left of the life I once had. I hired a nanny to care for Zach and Zoe before and after school. She came to the house to get them ready and walk them to school. I got dressed, packed my lunch and headed down the highway on my old commute. Trying to feel "normal," I turned on the radio. Thirty minutes later, there I was, at the front gate of Joyce Meyer Ministries. It was surreal to drive up to the building again. I waved at security as I always did. Parked in my normal spot. Said, hello to the guy at the front desk. Took the elevator to the third floor and walked into the executive office. All the ladies in our office cheered and came to greet me. They were always so sweet. There were lots of hugs as they welcomed me back. Other than their greeting, everything was as it had been sixteen months prior. I opened the door to my office and sat down at my desk to see all my belongings just as I had left them more than a year before.

It was like nothing had changed. And yet, everything had changed. My whole world had changed. But here I was in what used to be a daily routine. I desperately wanted to go back to business as usual. I needed to feel like I could put something in my existence back together again. I plugged in my computer and started going through emails. I had kept up with them while I was out, but I hadn't really cleaned things up. So, off I went. I was back to work, cleaning out my inbox.

In the next few days I had to look for things to do. I had some meetings. I got asked to do a few things I used to do. But for the most part, there wasn't much there for me. They didn't seem to have a place for me.

My responsibilities outside of Fuzed Worship had been pieced out to several different people. The ministry had to keep moving while time stood still in my world. I thought maybe they were easing me in and letting me readjust. Surely there was some big new projects waiting for me. There was always an endless sea of projects. But all I had was busy work.

Finally, Dan Meyer asked to have a meeting with me to talk about the state of Fuzed Worship. He asked me to meet him at a park. We sat on a bench and began a long conversation. We faced the truth that with everything that had happened, I wasn't in a place to tour as a single dad. On top of that, the ministry had to fill the conference dates a year in advance. Even if I could travel, it would be over three years in total that I was off the tour. Our record sales had pretty much dried up. I hadn't even seen the band in almost two years. Dan already knew what I was waking up to see. We had to make the decision to dismantle Fuzed Worship. We had a dream once, in his garage. We were writing songs together about the mission field. Now it was dying, too. I tried to hide my emotions as I was sick of being "that guy." I wanted to be strong and keep my chin up. We did our normal bro hug, talked about how much we loved our trucks, then we drove off. On my way home, I came to the harsh realization that I would need to start the process of grieving another loss. The loss of living the dream. The fact that cancer had taken even more from me than Dana was starting to settle in.

A few months went by with me filling time making phone calls, deleting Fuzed Worship accounts online and looking for things to do. I kept hoping there was some kind of new role or workload coming. But it didn't. In those months the kids and I got in a routine. The nanny did their homework with them. I grocery shopped and made dinners. We were doing it. We were living a new life.

We went on our trip to New York, started talking to Amy, and of course, got married. I talked to the Meyers through all of my decisions with Amy. They were family, and I needed to make sure I wasn't crazy. Joyce gave us her blessing. Dan Meyer and I went and picked out the ring, together. They tried to support me wherever they could. They were very gracious. But, in the end, there was another harsh reality that everyone could see, but me. Maybe I was in denial, but I couldn't imagine the ministry not having a place for me. We would figure it out together. I was a veteran employee. I had been there since I was a kid. We had a twenty-two-year history. It was just a few short months after I married Amy. We had just built a new life together. Was it possible that I was losing my job?

The fear of another great shift in my world began to consume me. I asked to meet with Dan Meyer again. We both shared our hearts.

"Dan," I began, "This is the only place I've ever worked. This is the only thing I know how to do."

"I know bro, but I also know God will make a way for you. I just really feel He has something new in store for you."

In truth, there simply wasn't a place for me at the ministry after being gone for so long during the cancer. He encouraged me to look for a new opportunity and said to take all the time I needed. Pray about it. I drove home from the meeting in shock.

I called Amy and broke the news to her. We both knew some kind of change was coming for me. But I kept assuring her I would have a job at the ministry for the rest of my life. But here I was - officially jobless. Amy was very comforting as usual and encouraged me not to panic. She always has a way of calming my soul. We knew that God had a plan.

In the weeks to come as I broke the news to people, everyone kept saying God must want to do a new thing in me. I knew the Father was moving me into a new season. He clearly had a plan in all this. But it was a lot to process. I could not see a new path, nor did I have the internal capacity to dream of one. I was stuck in what felt like a twilight zone. I couldn't go back. I couldn't move forward. So much loss and change coupled with the beauty of an entirely new life was requiring more faith from me. I didn't think I was emotionally ready for another massive shift. After all we had endured as a family, could we handle me being jobless for the first time in my life? The Meyers gracious again. They said they would patiently wait for me to figure out my next move, even if it took a year. But I couldn't ask any more of them after all they had done for us. I couldn't expect them to create a place for me. I put in my thirty-day notice and stepped into the unknown with the Father.

We had a rather somber going away party. One by one the staff came to congratulate me and say goodbye. I wasn't sure what I was being congratulated for. People tried so hard to be encouraging, but what could they say?

"Hey...sorry your wife died and now you have no job."

"So... good luck picking up all the shattered pieces of your life."

Everyone had so many questions. Where are you going? What made you resign? Are you going on a solo tour with your music? Man... this is crazy, are you sure you're ready for more change?"

I just froze and tried to pretend I knew what I was doing. The only thing I could figure out in a such a short time was that I may go work at the funeral home with Amy. She felt called to it and made great money. Maybe God could use our story to comfort other grieving people? Sure, that sounds like a plan. But I didn't have a clue. I was shell shocked. All I heard were mortar rounds going off in my head as one by one people fired questions at me. I was going back to the battlefield, unwillingly and completely unhealed.

On my last day, I packed all my stuff in boxes and loaded it into my truck. I drove away from the front door and couldn't hold back the tears. The driveway of the ministry has an epic view. It's a long winding road lined with flags from all the nations the ministry has outreaches in. As I drove down the hill on what feels like a very presidential mile, I just wept and prayed. I thanked God for all He allowed me to do there. I had a good run, but I had never felt so lost in my life. In all honesty, the absolute grief and pain that flooded my soul in the months to come almost took me down for the count.

I had fought so valiantly with Dana. We were a pillar of strength in the face of horrible loss. But I had now been drained of that strength. I couldn't find it. There were days when all I could do was weep for an hour and plead with the Father for guidance. I could feel the waves of depression coming in the morning as I scrambled to get my family out the door before, I broke down. As the last school bus drove away and I was finally alone, I would fall to the floor. Screaming at God, I would beg Him to speak to me. I would beg Him for an answer to the question of why He saw fit to strip me of everything I'd ever known as security and love. In my despair, I could not hear Him. All I could hear was the raging winds of the storm in my soul.

Our counselor referred to it as, "compounded grief." Like giant waves of life beating you down. Just when you think you are coming up for air and rebuilding, you get hit once again. It felt like more than I could bear. Only Jesus could hold me together. As if the grief from fifteen months of watching Dana pass away weren't enough, now I had to grieve all of this. The Father wanted me to grow in trust once again. It felt cruel of Him to ask all this of me, but I had to believe He had a plan for it all. He was radically uprooting everything I counted on in my life.

I just wanted to live and be in love. I felt this beautiful release from grief after Dana passed. I felt the worst was behind me.

Now I was going through yet another storm. My faith was being tested and sharpened once again. Joyce Meyer Ministries was more than a job to me. It was the only job I had ever known. Dana and I spent our entire life together pouring into that ministry. It was compounded loss. It was a loss of security and community. It was the loss of Fuzed Worship and all that it meant to me and others. It was the loss of the only way I knew how to provide for my new family. It was the loss of many long-term friends,

115

church family and relationships. I had so many unanswered questions for God.

Chapter 13

LEAVING THE LITTLE BLUE HOUSE

Blessed are those who mourn, for they shall be comforted
Matthew 5:4 (ESV)

With the family going down to one income, I had to sell the little blue house as quickly as possible. I had let it sit empty for a few months while Amy and I put our new life together. But Amy and I could not afford two mortgages now. The time had come for me to close that chapter of my life for good. I had never finished some of the final touches of the rehab. I would need to spend a day there to get it ready to list. The memories in that house would not be an easy thing to face. I'll never forget the day I drove to the little blue house for the last time.

The old streets of Saint Charles are so quaint. A far cry from the shiny new suburbia we lived in now. With the windows down, I could hear the crackle of left-over fall leaves beneath my tires. The breeze was warm and smelled of new beginnings and flowers in bloom. I needed to feel the pulse of that town again. St. Charles used to somehow calm the storms in me, bring

117

me peace. Something about the old architecture and historic community just felt right to my soul. I loved the huge trees draping over broken sidewalks and one-hundred-year-old houses dressed in beautiful textures and charm. Then there was Main Street with its coffee houses, antique stores and the vintage soda shop Zoe and I frequented on Daddy Daughter dates. The walks to and from school every day in the fall are forever etched in my memory as some of the most precious times in my life. The schoolhouse looks like one out of an old classic movie, complete with red brick, a two-story library filled with books and a crossing guard out front. It's picture perfect Americana. The Father was so faithful to bring us to St. Charles. But could I find that peace again? Now, those streets made me feel anxious and sad. Like a warrior looking back at the field of an epic battle, the smoke and embers still glowing in the ruble of my broken past. I couldn't explain what it stirred in me. But it felt more like fear than peace.

Pulling up to the curb, I put my truck in park and kept the engine running. It had been four months since the kids and I moved out. But it felt like twenty years. Staring up the hill the old house sat on, I began to dread the next several hours. Every sight and sound seemed so heightened and intense. I was stuck. Part of me so desperately needed to go back and close this chapter of our life. But the rest of me wanted to run as far from the pain as possible. I'm not sure how long I sat there, but I eventually got out of my truck and stood on the sidewalk for a bit. I can do this. I have to do this. But why, why now? Why after all I've been through, do I have to come here and deal with this? I grabbed ahold of the rot iron rail and held it tight, then slowly climbed the two flights of stairs to the front porch. As I turned to look back, my mind raced to the fall of the previous year when this little yard was filled with people in conversation about days passed. They were reliving moments with Dana and telling stories of all the times she made them laugh, cry and feel the pain of what she was enduring.

But now, here I was, standing in the peaceful breeze of spring and watching the redbuds fall from the small tree the kids used to climb. As the wind chimes sang, all I could do was stare at the heavy wooden door that stood between me and all my grief. Grabbing the handle, I wondered if I had it in me to spend the day in this empty house that was such a shelter to my family. It was so beautiful, but I didn't want to endure seemingly endless hours finishing the projects we started together.... alone. But what else did I have to do? I was jobless for the first time in twenty-two years and I had to sell that place. This is more than I felt my heart could bear.

There had to be something there for me. The Father started speaking. The waves of chaos in my soul were calming down.

I heard Him say, "I'm here Nate. Follow me through the door of all the pain you left here months ago."

I reluctantly squeezed the handle, walked in and trusted His voice. I needed to let Him open my wounds and heal them completely. That old door made a hollow, clunking noise every time it opened, such a familiar sound. It was like it triggered something in my mind, sending me into the realm of the past. The weathered wooden floors creaking beneath my feet like a weary ship at sea. The scent of the old house filling my nostrils. The beautiful archways and remodeled kitchen we labored on for months, now echoed with an empty silence. Sights, sounds and smells were rushing through me. I remember this. My, how things have changed in my life. Whirlwinds of beauty, trial and coarse altering chaos have blown me into a new reality. I know it's His goodness that has led us this far. But what shall I make of all that's shattered within me? The Father's voice led me forward. We began our journey through my wounded soul.

I stood for what seemed like an eternity in the entryway, gazing into the main living area of the little blue house. Memories began flooding in. The kids playing games in the floor. Dana... asleep in the chair under piles of blankets, stocking cap on her balding head. She could never get warm after her treatments. The overwhelming anxiety of the panic attacks I used to have swept in as my heart began to race. Then came the tunnel vision and nausea. All those late, sleepless nights, standing at that sink, cleaning feeding tubes and prepping her meds. I can't believe I made it through it all. I could see and feel all that pain and anxiety again.

Dinner placed on the countertop by loving folks that just wanted to help. Thank God for them. They always brought desert. I gained so much weight. Waves of emotion kept sweeping over me. As the anxiety subsided, I began to walk down the hall toward our children's rooms. The nightly scenes of bedtime prayers and tea parties played like a movie before me.

They asked such gut-wrenching questions.

"How can I love a God that's killing my mommy?"

"Daddy, who will be my mom if Mommy dies?"

It felt so real, and yet I knew I was far removed from it all. It felt pure and necessary for my soul. But as I turned to the left and saw the stairs my calm turned to dread. Not there. I won't do it. All the repairs and painting needed are on the bottom two levels. I need not go to the third floor. But the Father gently guided me once again. We began the climb, together.

A scene rushed in of the day she fell and tumbled down the stairs to the hall below. I could see her there, in the fetal position, crying out in pain.

"I hate these stairs, Father! I hate them!"

They were old and steep. She was too weak to use them. I later had them completely demolished and replaced with the sturdy, safe ones I now climbed. Those stairs were a source of stress and agony I did not want to revisit. I sprinted up and down them day and night as a makeshift nurse caring for Dana in ways I was not qualified for. More sadness happened at the top of them than I wanted to see again. But onward we climbed, despite the pain.

Time stood still as I made the turn and stepped into the master bedroom. It was bare and empty now, but in my mind's eye she lay there helpless. Scene after scene came to me as I processed all I had endured in the last fifteen months of our nineteen years together. I.V. poles and boxes of medical supplies stacked in the corners with nurses, family and friends, kneeling by her bedside. The sounds of her crying and sobbing in pain swept over me. I was overwhelmed with that helpless feeling I had when I could do nothing to fix her. I recalled the many talks we had when she worried about the kids and me after she was gone. She was determined to have every aspect of our life in order before she left for her eternal journey. She was afraid we couldn't do life without her.

Then I saw the picnic pizza parties on blankets in the floor with the kids. We could have a couple hours of peace. They just wanted to be next to her as much as possible, never knowing if it would be the last time she would hold them. She was so rarely awake for them to have that. I had dealt with much of my own grief in stages throughout her decent into the unthinkable dread of death at thirty-seven. But the more recent hits I had taken as a man broke me in ways I did not know how to process.

To lose my career and financial stability just a few short months after standing next to her gravesite with my children was more than I could take. I

121

lost so many friends and all the beautiful support we had. A tsunami came crashing down on our already broken vessel. It felt like we were sinking. The sun that was finally shining again went dark as another cloud overtook its light. So quickly the calm and relief of making it through the darkest of nights was swept away by yet another epic wave. At last I fell to the floor in the spot she once laid and wept uncontrollably. I wept for her, my knees in my chest like a child in the womb I shook and moaned in the pain. I wept for our children. I wept for all the beautiful souls that journeyed with us so fearlessly. I wept for me.

I finished all the repairs that day. The little blue house that was once our refuge and sturdy vessel in the storm was now spotless and ready for a new family's journey. I needed to sail on. As I walked out the back door for the last time, I thanked the Father for all He had seen us through. I thanked Him for the love, joy and yes, the pain that we all carried. It made us better and drew us to Him in ways I can't explain.

I locked the door behind me and walked through the peaceful backyard to gaze up one last time at the giant walnut tree. Its base was the backdrop for evening fires with so many talks of love and biblical counsel when we so desperately needed it. My church brothers and I drew ever close in the warmth of those fires as we talked about Jesus, grace and our love for sound theology. That giant tree shaded the entire yard and housed a million squirrels we used to shoot out of it with a BB gun. They were cute, but they were such a nuisance.

I paused to catch one last scene. The patio was circled with ladies, me and the kids. Razors and scissors in hand, Dana's golden locks fell to the ground. It was the day she revealed her new *"cancer patient"* look before her chemo started. She cried. We all cried. Then suddenly, it stopped. The visions were gone. My new reality was before me as the warm spring winds caught my sails. I had to keep moving. There was a new unchartered life ahead – a new adventure. I closed the gate behind me to walk one last time down the old alleyway. I never looked back.

Chapter 14

A LIFE OF LOVE

And now these three remain: faith, hope and love.
But the greatest of these is love.
1 Corinthians 13:3 (ESV)

In the months to come after my resignation from the ministry, and selling the little blue house, I didn't know what to do. I didn't know who to be, or how to be. My father was always in real estate and ministry. I thought maybe I would follow his path. I got my real estate license and signed with a local broker. It gave me something to focus on. My sweet family cheered me on as I put on my suit and headed out the door each day. It felt so foreign. Is this who I am now, a real estate guy? I felt like I was living someone else's life. I woke up one day in a new bed, lying next to a new wife, with new kids, in a new house, in a new neighborhood, with new neighbors, a new car in the driveway, a new job, a new boss, new friends, and new extended family. The weight of what God had called me to felt incredibly daunting. My personal battle with trusting God began to take a toll on me. I lost 25 pounds. My face was sinking in. I didn't look healthy. God was with me, but He was building something new in me. He was teaching me so much about myself. He was challenging the man I thought I wanted to be.

On my first day as an agent, I met two people. From a list of hundreds of houses for sale across the city, I picked these two. I didn't know why. I didn't have much reason other than they were in the price range I was allowed to pursue on my first day. They happened to be near Joyce Meyer Ministries which was forty minutes from my home. The drive was the same drive I had made while being employed there. Emotions began to stir in me. I could feel that God was about to show me His love and grace in this season.

The first home I went to belonged to an older Christian couple. As the husband began to share his story, I was amazed. His wife had battled cancer as well. Even more peculiar, after her battle, he wrote a book about it. Could this be? What kind of coincidence is this? I was dreaming of the day I would have the courage to start the intro to this book. I knew one day I would push through and start typing these pages. But I didn't have the courage yet. Now, here was a man who had lived it and done it. I was so encouraged. God was smiling on me. He was giving me hope in the wilderness. I left with a sense of wonder as I drove about fifteen miles to the next home. It was a small home, listed *For Sale by Owner*. I was there to try and get the listing for our agency. A young woman came to the door and gave me the tour. When we got to the finished basement, I began to tell her a bit of my story and how I got into real estate.

She stopped and said, "I'm sorry, what? Did you look me up online or something?"

I said, "No, of course not. Why would you ask that?"

As she began to tell me her story, I couldn't believe my ears. She had married a widower just three months after his late wife had passed. They only dated for a month before marrying. Everyone thought they had lost their minds. They lost a lot of friends as a result. There were children involved. I just stood and looked at her for a second. I didn't know what to say.

I finally said, "Well... I absolutely did not look you up online. What a bizarre coincidence! What are the odds that we would meet and share such a unique story?"

She just stared at me with this puzzled look on her face. I honestly don't think she believed me. I don't know that I would have believed me either. We encouraged each other to stay strong as I left. Needless to say, I did not get the listing that day. I think the whole thing was too much for her. She didn't know what to make of it. But, for me, it was a sign from the Father. He was with me. I had no idea what I was doing, or why He was taking me down this path. But He was with me. He was up to something. In His great love for me He was giving me signs along the way. He was taking me through another storm. Only this time, His will was to require me to stand on my own two feet. His aid and comfort were certainly there, but almost at a distance. He was further securing the strength He had placed within me. The question was, would I walk in that strength, or would I falter.

I pulled my new family close. Kids and dogs everywhere, it was quite the adjustment from our old life. There was this beautiful feeling of new beginnings and love all around. Yet, there was this sense of a vicious attack upon us. It felt like we were being sheltered in a war. There was an enemy, and he did not want us to be together. It was as if he couldn't harm us, but he was certainly trying. Opinions of what we should do, and how we should do it were constant. Accusations that this love was not real or somehow dirty and scandalous were a hurtful, regular assault.

One morning, in the haste of our morning routine, Amy looked at me with a very puzzled look on her face.

I said, "What's the matter baby?"

She said, "Don't freak out. But there's a lump on my breast."

In horror, my mind raced to all the horrible implications of that statement. God, no. We cannot survive another unexpected twist in our journey. I immediately held her, and we prayed. In my heart, I knew it was ok. But my mind was such a battlefield. We booked a doctor's appointment and got an inconclusive diagnosis. That led to another appointment and some testing. My soul was restless. Seeing Amy in hospital gowns and hospital beds, just like Dana. Wandering the same echoing halls that I sprinted down in agony that day I broke from the pain. This cannot be.

Not again. I needed another breaking point to let it all out. There were days when it was all I could do to get Amy and the kids out the door in the morning, so I could drop to my knees before the Lord. I held back the tears just long enough to see them off. But then the tears came like a flood. Finally, I had my moment, my breaking point with the Father. I dropped Zach and Zoe off at the private school they attended in our past life for an event. The history we had there was the trigger my soul needed.

I drove my truck to a secluded section of the parking lot, got out, dropped to my knees and screamed at the top of my lungs at the Father. "Where are You. Why are You doing this? What do You want from me?"

The tears began to pour out of me like a flood. I held out my hands, looked up to the sky, and let them flow. Finally, peace began to wash over me. I was fully surrendered. God began to speak. He reminded me of all the things He had spoken to me about my life with Amy. He asked me why I still could not trust Him.

127

I repented for my lack of trust as He reminded me of a faithful word I had received from Dave Meyer, Joyce Meyer's husband. Amidst the hugs and tears at the end of the funeral, the Meyer family came up to greet me. Dave Meyer said he had been praying for me all morning and really felt he had a word from God for me.

In tears he said, "Nate, you have lost the love of your life, but God is going to give you a life of love."

In that moment, the possibilities in those words seemed so far away and almost impossible to conceive. I couldn't see all that the Father would do so quickly. I couldn't see the amazing amount of love He was about to grant me. But I held on to this hope of a life of love. I prayed it would be so.

Now, in the parking lot crying out to God, I could see it. God had granted us that life of love. He was putting us through some tests to secure us in it. He was building a beautiful foundation for us to stand on. We were facing so much opposition right from the start, so that in tough seasons in the future we can rejoice and know that God will always be faithful. I stood up, revived with revelation from the Father, reminded of His faithfulness. To further secure this revelation I called Pastor Mike and told Him what we were facing. Once again, He had a word from God for me. He spoke of the epic battle that England faced against Nazi Germany in WWII. In that fight, London was ablaze in war as Hitler sent bombers over the city.

In a speech to the nation, Winston Churchill proclaimed, "Let us therefore brace ourselves to our duties, and so bear ourselves, that if the British Empire and its Commonwealth last for a thousand years, men will still say, 'This was their finest hour.'"

Mike said, "Nate, you are like Winston Churchill. You may be in a fierce battle, but this will be your finest hour. These are the trials that make great men great, and you are a great man. Rest in God's plan."

That was so what I needed to hear. I had lost my identity in the chaos. This was my new resolve. We would not only make it through this fight, but we would storm the gates and take hold of this "life of love" we were promised. We were victorious in Christ. God was at work in us and through us.

After several sleepless nights the tests came back from Amy's doctors. They revealed some scar tissue that had formed in her chest from a surgery she had when she was younger. All was well. There would be no cancer. There would be no treatments. She just needed a surgery to repair the scars of her past. But why the cancer scare? Why did I have to face that terror, walk those halls again, wait for test results, see her in those hospital gowns like Dana? I may never have answers, but I know there was a strengthening happening in Amy and my resolve. We were commissioned by the sovereign hand of God to be together. This entire journey was His story unfolding. It was His will for us. Something amazing was just over the horizon, through the smoke and bombs of battle.

As I write, Amy and I have been married two and a half years. I am astonished at all that has happened and the truth in this word from the Father, through Dave. Today I read my journal entry from Dec 3, 2015, less than a week after our first date. The things that I said in it, that I felt were the Father speaking to me, brought me to tears of joy. I saw all that God would do in our children through our marriage. I saw the absolute joy that would be ours in the future. I reminded myself to read this entry and take heart in tough times ahead. I confirmed that this love was from the Father. He was going to use our marriage in ways I couldn't even conceive in that moment. Now, just over two years later, after many trials, I see it not only in my heart, but in reality. The father has truly granted us a life of love. Healing that we'll never grasp the fullness of this side of eternity. It's precious and overwhelms us with goodness. I wrote in my journal, that many trials were ahead, but the covenant of marriage would cover us. The Father would shelter and sustain us. Oh, how true that has been.

A life of love. Love is so powerful. The bible says, it covers a multitude of sins. Out of faith, hope and love; love is the greatest.

Above all, keep loving one another earnestly, since love covers a multitude of sins. 1 Peter 4:8 (ESV)

And now these three remain: faith, hope and love. But the greatest of these is love. 1 Corinthians 13:3 (ESV)

Love covers us. It wipes away tears and pain and yes, the love of Christ, through His blood even wipes away our sin. As I embrace this new life of love, I can't even express to you what it has done. We are so healed, restored and covered with goodness. It is truly breathtaking. God has been so incredibly faithful. He has mended so much of what has been broken. I can't even begin to understand the chain of events that has brought us all together. But God is working all things together for our good. Everywhere we turn in our home there is love to be seen, and thankful for.

Somehow, Amy and the kids talked me into adopting two cats. I have never been a fan of cats and couldn't imagine how they would blend with our giant dogs. But even they have become a blended family. As soon as a kid in our home sits down, there is an animal ready to greet him or her and love on them. The cats lay with the dogs. Kids snuggle in bed with their furry friends. We sit at a giant table for dinner every night and have talks of the highs and lows from our day. We have ballgames and church on the weekends. There are daily fights between siblings over toys and who gets to sit next to mom. It's one big, happy, messy, blended bunch of beautiful chaos.

Many nights I will be sitting on the couch in a giant pile of kids, dogs, cats and deafening laughter as I hear the Father quietly whisper, "A life of love, Nate. A life of love."

MORE THAN ALL - THE GLORIES

By Nate Edmonds, Josh Bronleewe, Benji Cowart
(From the More than All the Glories Worship Project)

I have seen You in the darkest night of mourning
Felt You when my sorrow had no end
Even when the silence tried to call me lonely
I knew that I was held inside your hand
More than all the glories in the heavens
Boundless as the love that's in Your heart
More than all the drops that fill the oceans
Countless as the galaxies and stars
Oh, that's how good, that's how good,
that's how good You are
I can thank You for the questions still unanswered
Praise You for what I can't understand
I will revel in the mystery of Your goodness
Lift my hands surrendered to Your plans
Oh, that's how good, that's how good,
that's how good You are
I will rise up and praise You in the valley
For Your great love reaches to the sky
I will cry out and worship in the shadows
For Your goodness will always be my light

132

Chapter 15

MORE THAN ALL THE GLORIES

And we know that for those who love God all things work together for good,
for those who are called according to his purpose.
Romans 8:28 (ESV)

More than all the glories. It's the most beautiful and poetic way I knew to describe the love and goodness of God in suffering. Living this life of love, He has granted us is glorious. Feeling His comfort in the darkest night of mourning is glorious. Sensing His presence right in the middle of a season where it feels like sorrows have no end is glorious. Watching my children grieve well and receive healing from Christ was glorious. Watching a woman slip into eternity, knowing she is in Christ, sealed in His love forever was glorious. That's where we have come from. The things Zach, Zoe and I saw were tragic and awful. The things Amy has been through break my heart and make me angry all at the same time. Owen, Mason and Heidi wading through the brutal waters of a broken family and instability at home is a tough thing for little kids. Owen's Dad lives all the way in Canada. Mason and Heidi spend half their life with their dad and half with us. Those are hard situations to navigate. But the Father has held us. He has secured us in His love and in this life of love. His goodness is indescribable. Dana is in eternity with God. She doesn't miss us, and we are thriving in a new life. There's healing for us all, rather here and now, or in eternity with Christ. Healing is ours.

One day, I hope to be able to tell more of Amy's story. She endured unthinkable things in her past. The woman she has become could only happen by the grace of God. She is the most precious gift I have ever received. Together, Amy and I, five kids, two giant dogs and two cats, live the most beautiful life, every day. It's not perfect. But it is full of Gods glory and grace. Our children are thriving, flourishing and blooming in this new life of love. They all have straight A's in school. They play and do chores together. When I get my guitar out to practice, the two youngest kids we lovingly call "the babies" love to join me. Little Mason grabs his guitar and imitates my every move, even putting the pick in his mouth to finger pick when I do. It's precious. When little Heidi crawls up in my lap and asks me to read her a book, it melts my heart.

This weekend she snuggled up next to me on the couch and said "Nate, Nate" …. that's her name for me… "I love you, Mommy and my daddy the most."

For a blended family, nothing could be more precious than those words.

Amy and Zoe are like two peas in a pod. They love being girly together. They put makeup on and hit the mall eager to find the perfect boots, so all the girls can match. In the summer, Zoe goes to work with Amy almost every day. She picks her clothes out based on whatever Mom is wearing, and off they go in pencil skirts and high heels. Amy and I are developing together as parents. We're learning how much we truly complement each other. Where one is weak, the other is strong. I said in my journal entry, when we first met, that God has put things in Amy and me that the other desperately needs. I wrote that He would use us to mend each other's hearts. I wrote these things less than a week after our first date. I couldn't have known any of this by natural means. But the Father showed them to me that morning.

Owen has become the ultimate big brother. He always looks to protect his four young siblings. God forbid, someone ever pick on them. They will see Owen's wrath. He is fourteen years old, five foot ten, and one hundred seventy pounds. His voice is changing now. He is officially taller than me. At some point every day he decides to lift me up and bear hug me. I can barely breath. He squeezes so tight.

Zach and Zoe cheer when Amy says, "We have the babies this weekend."

It amazes me when I see how Zoe helps take care of the babies. What a gift to us all in our grief and struggle to adapt to the waves and changing tides of our life together. We have beautiful talks in a circle in our living room and work out any issues that arise. In one of those talks we asked each kid what we could do better as stepparents. The things they said were breathtaking. Amy was so blessed by Zach's comment.

He said, "Nothing Mommy, you are the best stepmom I could ask for."

In a recent school project, Zach was asked to write about someone that has had an impact on his life. He wrote the sweetest letter about his mom, Amy.

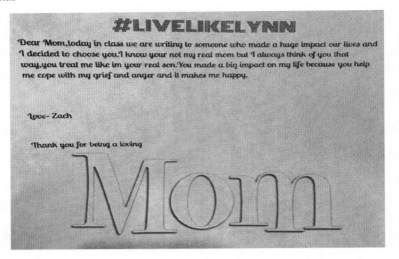

#LIVELIKELYNN

Dear Mom, today in class we are writing to someone who made a huge impact our lives and I decided to choose you. I know your not my real mom but I always think of you that way, you treat me like im your real son. You made a big impact on my life because you help me cope with my grief and anger and it makes me happy.

Love- Zach

Thank you for being a loving

Mom

Wow. That is restoration. That is glorious. Yes, Zach and Zoe call Amy, Mom or Mommy. That was their choice. They came to Amy and me on their own and said that was what they wanted to do. Is that not healing? Read the pages of this book and see the hell those kids went through. Think about how beautiful it is that they love Amy so much now and feel so loved by her that they want to call her Mommy. It's astonishing and an answer to many prayers, including Dana's. God is faithful when we give our suffering back to Him in glory.

Before I married Amy, I asked for Owen's blessing.

He said, "Yes, Nate, I know in my heart, you are a good man."

He had known me less than a month.

Early on, in one of our family talks, he said, "I just want Nate to snuggle with me more."

He was twelve years old at the time. I was blown away by that. Here is a kid that has been through a lot of twists, turns and changes in his life. He didn't have to trust me so quickly. Now, he loves me and wants me to tuck him in at night and snuggle with him. God has done so much, I can't help but stand amazed. God's goodness has spilled out in so many ways it's hard to take notice of them all. There are many more areas in our journey that need to be redeemed by it. But so many facets of our life have been washed in this love.

One situation that I never thought I'd encounter and honestly worried about was with Casey, Amy's ex-husband. I had no experience with blended families and didn't know how I would feel about all the dynamics of it. It was something I prayed a lot about when I first met Amy. Although Casey lives in Canada, Casey is very involved in our life. He's an amazing dad and calls Owen twice a day, every day. I respect that so much. He and his parents also stay with us when they come to get Owen and take him to Canada for holidays and summers. God has done an awesome work between us all. There's a lot of joy and love in our home when they are here. That is a blessing I never thought I'd be a part of.

On one of Casey's trips here, we had what Amy calls a "bromance moment." Casey and I really got to talk after a situation came up that we all needed to work through together. This ease from the Father was on us. It all worked out so smoothly. After our talk, Casey came into the room where me, Amy and Owen were. He thanked us for working through the situation with him. In tears he said, how thankful he was that I was in his son's life and how much respect he had for me. Earlier that day he even went so far as to say if Owen ever decided to call me dad as well, that he'd be honored by that. It would show him I was doing right by his boy.

I was stunned. I too, in tears, told him what an awesome dad he was. I said I brag on him all the time to people that ask about our situation. I said how amazing and honorable it was that he calls every day to be faithful to Owen. Few dads do those types of things these days. For Owen to witness us talking that day was incredible. For him to know we are all there to love and support him, and each other through this unique situation is healing. The Father's restoration surrounds us in our life.

God's goodness conquers every issue we encounter. Sins and sorrow from our past are redeemed in Christ. In His mercy, the Father allows this restoration to happen. Casey and his parents recently came to church with our whole crazy crew. I looked down the row at this family I never knew I'd be a part of. It was stunning. Everyone's hands were raised in worship together. A giant blended family seeing the restoration Christ brings, even to the messiest pieces of our life. One day, when our children face their own journeys, they will look back on all this and remember the Father's goodness. It will give them strength to conquer whatever comes their way.

So many people have embraced and loved us, including Dana's family. One by one I told them of our plans to marry and every one of them said, in tears, "We are with you guys." But so many others have struggled with it. We have felt so completely orphaned in some areas, but so covered and loved in others. When I sit back and take it all in, I see that as the Father has sheltered us in His goodness. Though storm after storm has come, within the walls of our home there is so much peace, joy and of course, love. This "life of love" shelters us. The Father's goodness has sustained us. But we have to stop and see it. We have to rise up and praise Him in the valley, knowing His great love is there. We have to cry out and worship in the shadows, knowing His goodness will guide us into the light. Then we can sing not only in faith, but with the promise before us…. "More than all the glories."

Chapter 16

ALIVE IN CHRIST

But God, being rich in mercy, because of the great love with which he loved
us, even when we were dead in our trespasses, made us alive together with
Christ—by grace you have been saved— and raised us up with him
and seated us with him in the heavenly places in Christ Jesus, so that in the
coming ages he might show the immeasurable riches of his grace in kindness
toward us in Christ Jesus. Ephesians 2:4-7 (ESV)

The scripture at the start of this chapter says that we are alive together with Christ. In the end, that is our story. This eternal perspective keeps us rooted and grounded in truth. The life of love is all around us as a reminder of the Father's goodness. "For His glory, by His grace" is still our family creed, yes, our battle cry. It is essential to the calling on our life together and brings clarity at times in our journey when things don't make sense to our natural mind. The plaque is still placed on our wall as a reminder of what God spoke as our mission in Him. No matter what my family faces, we know that we are part of a much larger story that the Father has asked us to tell. We simply must glorify Christ with our life. It's only by His grace that we can even begin to do that. Just as I told Zachary that day when he thought he hated God, we have a choice to glorify Jesus in this journey. There are things in this life we will not understand. But we must rest in grace and know that God is good. He is eternally and forever good.

Even as sorrows like sea billows roll, it can be well with our soul when we are alive in Christ. We are alive in Christ; therefore, we have everything we need to not only make it through the storm, but to live for the glory of Christ in the middle of the storm. That's what we chose to do as a family, to see the eternal perspective, trust in God's grace, and live for His glory.

Question one of The Westminster Catechism asks this – "What is the chief and highest end of man?"

And the answer… "Man's chief and highest end is to glorify God, and fully enjoy Him forever."

As I grow in Christ and have lived more life than I ever thought I would, I find this to not only be true; but I can see it unfolding in my own story. In the end, God is after two things – His glory and our joy. If I am alive in Christ, and living for His glory, then in that my joy will be found. I can say with confidence that my joy is truly found there. When I look at the life the Father has granted me, Amy, and our children, all I see is the hand of a faithful God. Two stories of complete brokenness colliding in Christ and somehow, filled with joy. He showed us His great love in that collision. Only the hand of Father could orchestrate the overwhelming number of events it took to bring us all together. He is the author and finisher of our faith. He is good. In all our brokenness and weakness, He is strong.

The Father is writing a new chapter in our story and spring has come. We are in a true season of new beginnings and fresh life is being breathed into our family. We are all growing in grace and understanding for each other's past. We eat dinner as a family every night around a huge dining room table. As we eat, the kids give us the highs and lows of their day. Owen goes off to Canada several times a year with his dad. The babies are back and forth each week from their dad's house to ours. Every birthday and Christmas, Zach and Zoe watch their videos from Dana and wear their new trinket before placing it in their memories box. Even on our worst days when it seems everyone is tired and not getting along as usual, we can't help but see the Father's goodness. We are alive, together, with Christ.

After a time of healing, God began to give me vision for a new life in ministry. About a year into my marriage with Amy, I found the courage to begin writing this book and dream of the "More Than All the Glories" worship project. The home Amy had purchased happened to be one exit away from Element Church, the church Dana and I attended before the storm. Day after day I would drive by Element on my way home and feel the Father pulling me back there. I will never fully understand all the moving puzzle pieces in our story. But, from my current perspective, on the other side of the storm, God called us to Matthias' Lot Church for a very specific purpose. It was a beautiful and gracious shelter for us in the storm. Community is a part of the DNA of that church. The Father used them in such profound ways that I will be forever grateful for. Then, after that storm had ceased, I was called back to Element Church.

I'll never forget the day Amy and I, and all the kids, walked back into the lobby. We were welcomed with open arms. So many people ran up and hugged us and introduced themselves to the new family. Apparently, a mass text went out that said "Nate Edmonds is in the lobby." A flood of staff and volunteers I worked with ran out to greet us. We felt so loved. We were back home.

In the weeks to come, we attended Element faithfully. We needed time to adjust. The services and rhythms of Element and Matthias are very different. About eight weeks in, I began to hear God speak. Amy had started encouraging me to get back on the platform and lead worship again. I had only led worship four times in the last three years. It was crazy that I went from constantly leading worship and being all in with my calling to almost never leading. It was like God stripped me of everything. I knew I wasn't healthy. I knew I needed to get back to my calling. But part of me didn't want to.

During worship one Sunday I heard God clearly say, "Nate, I brought you back for a specific purpose. I'm about to do a very special work here. I brought you back at just the right time."

Nathan Elder, an Executive Pastor at Element, began to gently approach me and invite me to be on the worship team. He was the worship pastor for several years, so he understood my calling well. With him and Amy encouraging me, I gave in. I started slow. I just played guitar. Then I led a song. Then they gave me a service in our smaller Fireside venue. Then it was Christmas at Element, our biggest production of the year. Then I was all in, leading worship in one of our venues twice a month.

Over the next several months, the Father moved in profound ways. Nathan said he wanted to have us over for dinner one night.

On the way to his home God spoke to me. "Nathan is going to ask you to be on staff at Element."

I told Amy and she got excited, "I guess we'll see what happens tonight. But please don't get your hopes up."

She knew how bad I was struggling doing real estate. God spoke to her one day in her morning prayer. She called me in, hugged me and cried. In that moment she spoke what she felt was the Father saying how much He loved me and how proud He was of me. She told me to quit real estate and take a short sabbatical until God opened a ministry door. I did it, and God moved. Literally as soon as we walked into their house the kids went one way, the wives went into the kitchen, and Nathan and I sat down for a talk on their couch.

First thing out of Nathan's mouth was…."so, I think God wants to bring you on staff at Element. I don't know how or for what. But it's going to happen."

I couldn't believe it. I literally just heard this from God and told Amy.

The rest is history. Over the next couple of months, we had meetings and interviews as God spoke to the rest of the executive staff. Before I knew it, I was in, but with no real title or direction. God, and the staff knew I needed time to heal. I was brought in as an Assistant Creative Pastor/Pastor in training. I was ordained by the church as a pastor and spent the next year leading worship, helping run the worship department and being a part of some creative strategies. Then something really special came along.

I was asked to be the worship pastor at the first satellite campus Element launched. Out of all the cities surrounding Saint Louis that this new campus could have been built in, guess where the Father led them to go? Saint Charles, just 1.8 miles from the little blue house. Week after week I was given the chance to pastor and lead the people of Saint Charles in worship. I was able to return to that city that was once such a beautiful shelter to our family and give back. So much redemption! So much life in Christ!

Once that campus was up and running, I was finally ready for my current role in ministry. I was promoted to Worship Pastor of Element Church. It's been such an honor to take this journey with Pastor Erik, the church staff and our congregation. I was accepted in my broken state. I was given the time to heal. God is truly moving in the worship experiences of our church. We are seeing new life and vision unfold. The worship team is dreaming of the future and starting to write songs for our church. It is a new day.

As if my completely new role wasn't enough, God began to move on Amy's heart as well. Life at the funeral home was beginning to weigh on her soul. She loved serving families there, but felt a change coming for her. A door opened up for her to take over half of the clientele from a successful insurance agency. It was a scary move for us as she would not know her income for quite a while. We prayed, felt peace and in our typical fashion, took the leap. In one hundred days, Amy got her licenses, found a staff, and started selling insurance. While she was doing that, I found a store front, headed up the construction, furnished it, and had all the signs installed. The client base she took over was from a faithful brother in Christ. Many of her clients are believers and church family. The kids can even take over the family business one day if they want. It is setting up a beautiful future for our family.

In all the joy that the Father has brought us, there is one blessing that might be my favorite. As one of my first pastoral duties, I was given the great honor of baptizing my family and several others. Zachary was baptized at Element when he was younger. But for several months, Zoe had been asking to be baptized. This sparked a lot of conversations in our family about what it means to be baptized. These conversations led us to discover that Amy and Owen had actually never been baptized. When Amy and I first started dating, Owen was sitting on the couch one day and explained to her that he had recently felt like sunshine had come into his heart. He asked to know more about God. A few weeks after our family's return to Element, he raised his hand in church and gave his heart to Jesus. Now, they all wanted to be baptized as a public display of their faith. The old man was being washed away, and a new life was "Alive in Christ." With all the church singing in worship and tears streaming down our faces, one by one I held Amy, Owen and Zoe in my arms and baptized them in the name of the Father, Son and Holy Spirit.

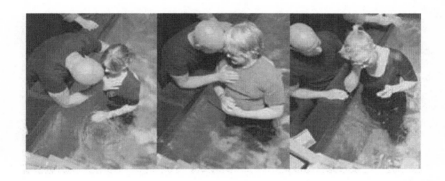

The redemptive nature of the Father on that day will forever reign in our hearts. It was breathtaking. We are all truly now *Alive in Christ*. He is our joy in suffering, the reason why we sing.

I wrote the song "Alive in Christ" with some faithful brothers in Nashville. This project ends in celebration. It expresses a heart of thankfulness for all that the Father has seen us through in Christ. We certainly have a cross to bear, but it's our treasure when we carry it for His glory. We were crushed, but not forsaken, bruised but not forgotten. Let these words sink in as our journey through this chapter of our story comes to an end.

ALIVE IN CHRIST

Nate Edmonds, Josh Bronleewe, Matt Armstrong

(From the More than All the Glories Worship Project)

This cross You gave I'll bear it, for Your glory is my treasure

All for You, All for You

I will soar on wings like eagles, I will run and not grow weary

All for You, All for You

I am crushed but not forsaken, I am bruised but not forgotten

Crucified but now I will rise

I am alive in Christ, I am alive in Christ

My joy in suffering, the reason why I sing

I am alive, I am alive

Every trial, every valley, I'll give glory to Your name

I live for You, I live for You

And Your presence is my passion

All Your ways are my good fortune

I long for You, I long for You

I am crushed but not forsaken, I am bruised but not forgotten

Crucified but now I will rise

I am alive in Christ, I am alive in Christ

My joy in suffering, the reason why I sing

I am alive, I am alive

I will sing of mercy

I will sing of wondrous grace

I will tell the story of how love took my place

I am alive, I am alive

Thank you, for taking this journey with me. I pray that our story proves God's love and faithfulness to you. I pray it grips your heart, and the Father uses it to grant you the faith to press on. I pray you see from an eternal perspective and let God be God in your story. Trust in Him, no matter what you are facing. Rise up and praise Him in the valley for His great love reaches to the skies. Cry out and worship in the shadows. For His goodness will always be your light. Let your heart sing... "More than all the glories in the heavens, boundless as the love that's in Your heart. More than all the drops that fill the oceans. Countless as the galaxies and stars.... that's how good You are."

Made in the
USA
Lexington, KY